ROYAL HA

THE UNOFFICIAL DEFINITIVE HISTORY OF QUEEN AND FREDDIE MERCURY

By Gary Ogden

TABLE OF CONTENTS

Chapter 1:
The Origins of Queen

BRIAN MAY'S EARLY LIFE AND MUSICAL BEGINNINGS

Brian Harold May, born on July 19, 1947, in Hampton, England, was deeply interested in music and science from an early age. His father, Harold, was an electronics engineer, and young Brian shared his father's fascination with technology. As a teenager, Brian was drawn to the guitar, but instead of buying one, he and his father famously built the "Red Special" guitar from scratch, using wood from a fireplace mantelpiece and bike parts. This guitar would go on to become iconic for its unique sound and would accompany May throughout his career.

Brian excelled academically and pursued a degree in physics at Imperial College London. Despite his scientific ambitions, music was always close to his heart. During his time at university, he co-founded the band *Smile* with Tim Staffell and drummer Roger Taylor. It was in this band that May began experimenting with layered guitar harmonies and the distinctive, intricate sound that would later define Queen.

ROGER TAYLOR: THE DRUMMER WITH A VOCAL EDGE

Roger Meddows Taylor was born on July 26, 1949, in King's Lynn, Norfolk. As a child, he displayed an interest in music and began playing the ukulele. But it wasn't until his teenage years that he switched to the drums. Taylor's influences ranged from jazz and swing to rock and roll, and he developed a style marked by heavy drumming and rhythmic complexity.

Roger moved to London to study dentistry at the London Hospital Medical College, but like May, he felt drawn to music. He joined *Smile* in 1968, contributing not only his powerful drumming but also his vocal abilities. His high-pitched harmonies would become a key feature of Queen's layered sound. Though *Smile* enjoyed some success, the group was still searching for its unique identity and future frontman.

FREDDIE BULSARA: ZANZIBAR TO LONDON

Freddie Mercury was born Farrokh Bulsara on September 5, 1946, in Zanzibar (modern-day Tanzania). He spent much of his childhood in India, where he received piano training and attended a British-style boarding school. Freddie's early exposure to classical music and rock 'n' roll had a significant influence on his later creative development. As a teenager, he formed a band called *The Hectics*, performing covers of rock hits.

In 1964, following political unrest in Zanzibar, Freddie's family moved to England, settling in Feltham, Middlesex. Freddie pursued a degree in art and design at Ealing Art College, a background that would later shape his bold stage persona and visual contributions to Queen's identity. His flamboyant style and deep appreciation for musical theatrics drew him into the London music scene, where he crossed paths with Brian May and Roger Taylor.

THE FORMING OF QUEEN

After *Smile* disbanded, Freddie, who had long been friends with May and Taylor, was invited to join them in 1970. By this time, Freddie had adopted the surname Mercury, symbolizing his larger-than-life persona. He pushed the group to embrace a more theatrical and diverse musical style, blending rock, opera, and intricate harmonies.

Freddie's arrival brought a newfound energy, and he had a clear vision for the band's image and direction. He insisted on the band having a name that reflected grandeur and drama, eventually settling on "Queen." Despite initial hesitation from Brian and Roger, Freddie convinced them that the name "Queen" represented an elegant yet bold identity, fitting the grandiose music they aspired to create.

JOHN DEACON: COMPLETING THE BAND

John Deacon, born August 19, 1951, in Leicester, England, was the final piece of the puzzle. A self-taught bassist, Deacon was known for his technical proficiency and low-key demeanor, which contrasted with the rest of the band's flamboyance. He studied electronics at Chelsea College in London and shared an interest in sound engineering.

In 1971, after several failed auditions with other bassists, May and Taylor met Deacon and immediately knew he was the right fit. Deacon's quiet professionalism balanced the band's more extroverted personalities, and his skills in electronics played a pivotal role in shaping Queen's distinctive sound, particularly in the studio.

EARLY INFLUENCES AND INSPIRATIONS

As Queen formed, the band members drew from a wide array of influences. Brian May's guitar style was rooted in the likes of Jimi Hendrix, Jeff Beck, and The Shadows, while Freddie Mercury was influenced by Liza Minnelli, Aretha Franklin, and Elvis Presley. Roger Taylor admired drummers such as Keith Moon of *The Who* and Mitch Mitchell of *The Jimi Hendrix Experience*, while John Deacon favored the precise, melodic bass lines of James Jamerson and Paul McCartney.

These eclectic influences were synthesized into something wholly unique. Queen aimed to fuse the virtuosity of progressive rock with the raw power of hard rock, and the theatricality of opera and musical theater.

EARLY GIGS AND REHEARSALS

In their early days, Queen played small gigs around London, often performing in empty clubs. These humble beginnings helped them refine their onstage dynamics, particularly Freddie's theatrical performance style. Brian's homemade Red Special guitar gave the band a signature sound that distinguished them from other rising acts.

By 1972, Queen had established a regular rehearsal space in Imperial College, where they honed their craft. They recorded a demo tape with De Lane Lea Studios in the hopes of landing a record deal. Their dedication to complex arrangements and multi-tracked harmonies marked them as innovators, though they would struggle to gain attention from record labels for a time.

SIGNING WITH TRIDENT AND EMI

After several rejections, Queen caught the attention of Trident Studios' management team, who signed them to a management and publishing contract. Although the deal had some limitations, it gave Queen access to high-quality recording facilities, which would be pivotal in shaping their early albums.

In 1973, Queen signed a record deal with EMI, marking the official beginning of their journey as professional recording artists. They quickly began work on their debut album, *Queen*, which blended heavy metal, progressive rock, and intricate harmonies. While the album didn't achieve immediate commercial success, it established Queen as a band with a unique sound and enormous potential.

Chapter 2:
Early Struggles and First Success

THE QUEST FOR A RECORD DEAL

In the early 1970s, despite their undeniable talent and unique sound, Queen struggled to gain traction in a music industry that was already brimming with established bands. The London rock scene was competitive, with artists like Led Zeppelin, Pink Floyd, and David Bowie commanding the spotlight. Record labels were hesitant to invest in new acts, especially one as eclectic as Queen, whose fusion of heavy rock, classical influences, and intricate harmonies was unlike anything on the airwaves.

After recording a few demos in 1971, Queen spent much of 1972 trying to secure a recording contract. Their live performances in small clubs were met with enthusiastic but modest audiences, and they faced rejections from several major record companies. Despite this, the band remained confident in their abilities, bolstered by Freddie Mercury's belief in their potential to achieve greatness.

A Breakthrough with Trident Studios

Their fortunes shifted when they crossed paths with Trident Studios. Trident, known for its high-quality recording facilities, had connections with major acts like The Beatles and David Bowie. Queen's demo tape caught the attention of Trident's co-owner, Norman Sheffield, who saw promise in their theatrical and ambitious sound.

While Trident didn't offer a record deal right away, they offered the band a management contract. This was a double-edged sword. On the one hand, it allowed Queen to use the state-of-the-art Trident Studios to record their music, which was crucial for a band with such complex arrangements. On the other hand, the management deal had financial limitations, offering little upfront payment and leaving Queen largely dependent on the success of their future albums.

Nonetheless, Queen took the opportunity, determined to make the most of the situation. The band entered the studio in late 1972, working tirelessly on their debut album, blending elements of progressive rock, heavy metal, and layered vocal harmonies. Freddie's visionary approach to songwriting, combined with Brian's innovative guitar work and the tight rhythm section of Roger and John, began to crystallize into a distinctive sound.

The Release of Queen (1973)

In July 1973, Queen's self-titled debut album, *Queen*, was released by EMI in the UK and Elektra Records in the United States. The album was a bold introduction to the band, featuring songs that showcased their eclectic influences and ambitious style.

Tracks like "Keep Yourself Alive" and "Liar" stood out for their combination of intricate guitar work, soaring vocals, and aggressive energy. "Keep Yourself Alive," the lead single, displayed Brian May's signature guitar tone and innovative use of harmonics, while "Liar" revealed Freddie Mercury's flair for dramatic storytelling and dynamic vocal range.

Despite their creative prowess, the album struggled to find commercial success. It received moderate airplay on radio stations, but sales were slow. Critics were divided: some praised the album's originality and technical prowess, while others found it too complex or difficult to categorize. Yet, this debut laid the foundation for what was to come.

Queen's live performances, however, began to gain traction. Audiences were captivated by Freddie Mercury's flamboyant stage presence, which blended theatricality and raw charisma. Dressed in extravagant outfits and interacting with the crowd in a bold, unapologetic manner, Freddie quickly became the focal point of Queen's live shows. His ability to engage an audience, paired with the band's tight musicianship, left a lasting impression on those who saw them live.

THE FOLLOW-UP: QUEEN II (1974)

Unfazed by the commercial underperformance of their debut album, Queen quickly returned to the studio to record their second album, *Queen II*. Released in March 1974, this album marked a significant evolution in the band's sound and approach to songwriting.

Queen II was a more ambitious and cohesive work, featuring greater complexity in both musical structure and lyrical themes. It was also a concept album of sorts, divided into two halves: the "White Side" (primarily written by Brian May) and the "Black Side" (largely composed by Freddie Mercury). This duality allowed the band to explore contrasting themes of light and darkness, good and evil, and fantasy versus reality.

Freddie's theatricality was on full display in songs like "Ogre Battle" and "The March of the Black Queen," which foreshadowed the epic, operatic style he would later perfect in *A Night at the Opera*. These tracks were filled with multi-tracked vocals, intricate arrangements, and dynamic shifts, pushing the boundaries of what rock music could achieve.

Brian May, meanwhile, continued to refine his guitar style, layering harmonized leads and experimenting with unconventional sounds. His track "Father to Son" showcased his love for orchestral composition within a rock context, while "White Queen (As It Began)" revealed his ability to craft hauntingly beautiful ballads.

Despite its creative strengths, *Queen II* was again met with mixed reviews. Some critics found the album overly ambitious and difficult to follow, while others praised its boldness and innovation. Commercially, it performed better than their debut, reaching number 5 on the UK Albums Chart, and began to attract a more dedicated fanbase. The album's single, "Seven Seas of Rhye," became Queen's first hit, reaching number 10 on the UK Singles Chart. This success gave the band a much-needed boost in confidence and credibility.

BUILDING MOMENTUM WITH SHEER HEART ATTACK (1974)

Later that same year, Queen took a more focused approach with their third album, *Sheer Heart Attack*, released in November 1974. This album marked a turning point in their career, as it combined the intricate musicality of their previous work with a more accessible, radio-friendly sound.

Sheer Heart Attack was a diverse album, showcasing the band's ability to tackle multiple genres. Tracks like "Killer Queen," "Stone Cold Crazy," and "Now I'm Here" demonstrated the band's versatility. "Killer Queen" in particular, written by Freddie Mercury, became a breakthrough hit, reaching number 2 on the UK Singles Chart and introducing the band to a wider audience.

The success of "Killer Queen" was pivotal. It was an art-pop masterpiece, blending glam rock with cabaret influences, and it highlighted Freddie Mercury's talent for writing catchy, sophisticated songs. The track's success extended to the United States, where it became Queen's first charting single, reaching number 12 on the Billboard Hot 100.

Sheer Heart Attack also received critical acclaim, with many praising its variety and energy. The album reached number 2 on the UK Albums Chart and number 12 in the US, establishing Queen as a major force in the rock world. It was also during this time that Queen's live performances began to reach new heights. Freddie's confidence as a frontman soared, and his relationship with the audience became more interactive and dynamic.

The band's stage shows became more elaborate, featuring a mix of visual theatrics, powerful performances, and tight musicianship. Queen was no longer just a promising band – they were becoming a rock powerhouse, capable of competing with the biggest acts of the era.

EARLY STRUGGLES WITH FINANCES AND MANAGEMENT

Despite their growing success, Queen continued to struggle with financial difficulties in their early years. The management contract with Trident Studios proved to be less favorable than the band initially realized, and they were often left with little to show for their efforts. This led to increasing tensions between the band and Trident's management, who they felt were taking advantage of them.

Freddie Mercury, in particular, was frustrated with the band's financial situation, feeling that their hard work wasn't being properly rewarded. The band began to explore ways to extricate themselves from the contract, eventually leading to a split with Trident in 1975. This decision would pave the way for Queen to take greater control over their career and finances.

SETTING THE STAGE FOR STARDOM

By the end of 1974, Queen had established themselves as one of the most exciting new bands on the rock scene. Their live performances were drawing larger and larger audiences, and they were beginning to gain a reputation as innovators, both musically and visually. The success of *Sheer Heart Attack* was a major turning point, and it gave the band the momentum they needed to push forward.

However, despite their rising fame, Queen was still searching for their defining moment. They were on the cusp of something great, but it wasn't until the following year that they would create the masterpiece that would change everything: *A Night at the Opera*. This would be the album that propelled Queen into global superstardom and cemented their place as one of the most influential bands of all time.

Chapter 3:
The Breakthrough:
A Night at the Opera

BREAKING FREE FROM TRIDENT: A RISKY MOVE

By 1975, Queen had grown frustrated with their financial situation under Trident Studios. Despite the commercial success of *Sheer Heart Attack*, the band was still receiving meager earnings due to the restrictive management contract. Freddie Mercury was particularly vocal about his dissatisfaction, often remarking that it was absurd for a successful band to be struggling financially.

Queen decided to make a bold move—they broke away from Trident Studios and hired John Reid, Elton John's manager, to represent them. This decision came with risks. Reid demanded full creative and financial control for Queen, which would cost them access to the high-end recording facilities at Trident, but the band felt it was the only way to gain the freedom they needed.

John Reid's entry marked a turning point for Queen. With a new management team that believed in their artistic potential and a renewed sense of purpose, the band was ready to take a huge leap forward. This set the stage for their next project, which would become not just a breakthrough for Queen, but a landmark in rock music history: *A Night at the Opera.*

THE VISION FOR A NIGHT AT THE OPERA

Sheer Heart Attack had solidified Queen's place in the rock world, but Freddie Mercury, Brian May, Roger Taylor, and John Deacon wanted more. They envisioned their next album as something grander—an opus that would blend their diverse musical influences, from rock to classical, with Freddie's flair for theatricality. The album's title, *A Night at the Opera*, was taken from the Marx Brothers' 1935 film of the same name, reflecting the album's mix of humor, drama, and sophistication.

The concept for *A Night at the Opera* was simple: no limits. The band wanted to push the boundaries of rock music, both sonically and thematically. They aimed for a lavish production with multiple layers of sound, intricate arrangements, and songs that ranged from playful to operatic. With an enormous budget for the time—reportedly around £40,000—the band set out to create an album that would be unlike anything the world had heard before.

At the heart of *A Night at the Opera* was Freddie Mercury's ambition to create something truly theatrical. Inspired by classical composers like Wagner and the operatic storytelling of bands like The Who, Freddie wanted to fuse rock music with the drama and grandeur of opera. His confidence in his vision was infectious, and the rest of the band, although initially unsure about some of the more outlandish ideas, trusted Freddie's instincts.

THE MAKING OF A NIGHT AT THE OPERA

Recording for *A Night at the Opera* began in August 1975 and took place over several months at various studios, including Rockfield Studios in Wales. The sessions were intense, as the band and producer Roy Thomas Baker worked tirelessly to bring their vision to life. The recording process was technically challenging and required a level of precision that was unheard of at the time.

The album's most famous track, "Bohemian Rhapsody," became the centerpiece of this ambitious project. Freddie Mercury had been working on the song for years, crafting it in pieces at the piano. The band had no idea at first how groundbreaking the track would become, but as they layered the vocals and guitars, it began to take on a life of its own.

The operatic section of "Bohemian Rhapsody" was particularly complex, with the band recording endless vocal overdubs to create a choir-like effect. At one point, there were so many vocal tracks layered together that the recording tape began to wear thin, pushing the limits of technology at the time. Freddie, with his perfectionist streak, demanded take after take until everything sounded exactly as he envisioned.

The track was a departure from anything Queen—or any other rock band—had ever done before. It blended ballad, opera, and hard rock into a seamless six-minute epic that defied convention. The song's structure was unconventional—there was no chorus, and it shifted between various musical styles in a way that should have made it incoherent, yet it worked brilliantly.

Beyond "Bohemian Rhapsody," the album featured a wide variety of musical styles. Brian May's "The Prophet's Song" was a nine-minute epic, inspired by his dreams and filled with layers of vocal harmonies and guitar solos. The song's haunting middle section, where Brian and Freddie's vocals echo over a sparse, apocalyptic soundscape, became one of the album's highlights.

John Deacon's contribution, "You're My Best Friend," was a light, pop-influenced love song, demonstrating the band's range and Deacon's understated songwriting talent. Meanwhile, Roger Taylor's "I'm in Love with My Car" was a gritty, hard-rock anthem that became a fan favourite, despite its offbeat subject matter.

Each member of the band brought something unique to the table, and *A Night at the Opera* reflected the diversity of their individual talents. The result was an album that felt cohesive despite its genre-hopping, largely because of the band's commitment to pushing the boundaries of what rock music could be.

THE RELEASE OF "BOHEMIAN RHAPSODY" AND ITS IMPACT

When *A Night at the Opera* was completed, the band faced a dilemma: which song should be the lead single? Freddie Mercury was adamant that "Bohemian Rhapsody" should be released as a single, despite its six-minute length, which was considered far too long for radio play at the time. Most singles were around three minutes, and record executives were skeptical that such an unusual song would receive airplay.

Queen took matters into their own hands. They handed an advance copy of "Bohemian Rhapsody" to influential DJ Kenny Everett, who famously teased listeners by playing snippets of the song, generating huge anticipation. When he finally played the full track on Capital Radio, the public's reaction was immediate and overwhelming. Radio stations around the UK started playing the song in full, and it quickly climbed the charts.

"Bohemian Rhapsody" spent nine weeks at number one on the UK Singles Chart, becoming one of the best-selling singles of all time. Its success defied industry norms, proving that audiences were hungry for something different. The song's groundbreaking music video, directed by Bruce Gowers, further cemented its place in history. The video, featuring the iconic shot of the band's faces in shadow, became one of the first music videos to receive heavy airplay on television, setting the stage for the MTV era that would follow.

CRITICAL AND COMMERCIAL RECEPTION OF A NIGHT AT THE OPERA

When *A Night at the Opera* was released in November 1975, it was an instant success. The album topped the UK Albums Chart and peaked at number 4 on the US Billboard 200. Critics praised the album for its ambitious scope, innovation, and musicianship, hailing it as a masterpiece. Even those who had previously been critical of Queen's theatricality were won over by the sheer audacity and brilliance of the album.

The album's commercial success was unprecedented for Queen. It went on to sell millions of copies worldwide and earned the band their first platinum record in the United States. More importantly, it catapulted Queen into the upper echelon of rock royalty, solidifying their place alongside the biggest names in music.

Beyond the commercial impact, *A Night at the Opera* also had a profound influence on the music industry. The album's use of multi-tracked vocals, layered guitars, and diverse musical styles pushed the boundaries of what a rock album could be. It showed that rock music could be artful, complex, and theatrical while still being accessible and commercially viable.

THE TOUR: BRINGING A NIGHT AT THE OPERA TO LIFE

After the album's release, Queen embarked on a massive tour to support *A Night at the Opera*. The tour, which began in the UK in late 1975 and continued into 1976, was a spectacle in itself. Queen's live performances had always been theatrical, but this tour took things to a new level. The band incorporated elaborate lighting, stage effects, and costume changes, with Freddie Mercury at the center of it all, captivating audiences with his magnetic stage presence.

Freddie's larger-than-life persona was in full force during this tour. Dressed in everything from a Zorro-like outfit to a sequinned leotard, he commanded the stage with a mix of camp and charisma, making every performance feel like a grand event. His ability to connect with the audience, even in massive arenas, was unparalleled, and Queen's live shows became legendary.

The band's technical precision on stage matched the ambition of their studio work. Brian May's guitar playing was as meticulous live as it was on record, and the harmonies, particularly in songs like "Bohemian Rhapsody" and "The Prophet's Song," were executed flawlessly. Queen's ability to recreate their complex studio sound in a live set, setting them apart from many of their peers.

LEGACY OF A NIGHT AT THE OPERA

"A Night at the Opera* was more than just a commercial success; it became a cultural phenomenon. "Bohemian Rhapsody" in particular took on a life of its own, becoming one of the most iconic songs in rock history. The track's lasting appeal was demonstrated decades later when it re-entered the charts in 1992, following its use in the film Wayne's World. Its continued relevance and frequent appearances in pop culture are a testament to its timeless quality".

The album also solidified Queen's reputation as one of the most innovative and adventurous bands in rock music. It proved that rock didn't have to be formulaic or confined to the conventions of the time. Queen had shown that there was room for experimentation, operatic grandeur, and theatricality in rock, paving the way for future generations of musicians to push the boundaries of the genre.

Chapter 4:
The Evolution of the Band's Sound

BUILDING ON THE SUCCESS OF A NIGHT AT THE OPERA

With the groundbreaking success of *A Night at the Opera*, Queen had cemented their place as one of the most innovative and popular rock bands of the 1970s. However, rather than resting on their laurels, Queen was determined to continue pushing musical boundaries. The band's unique ability to blend various genres—from hard rock to opera, ballads to progressive rock—had set them apart, but they were still hungry for more.

Freddie Mercury, in particular, was a driving force behind this desire to keep evolving. Never one to conform to expectations, Freddie was always eager to explore new creative avenues. Brian May, Roger Taylor, and John Deacon shared this passion for experimentation, and as a result, Queen's sound continued to evolve in exciting and unexpected ways.

The band's next project, *A Day at the Races* (1976), would take the ambitious approach of *A Night at the Opera* and refine it even further. While it may not have reached the same towering heights of its predecessor, *A Day at the Races* solidified Queen's identity as a band that thrived on versatility, unpredictability, and grandiose production.

A DAY AT THE RACES (1976): REFINING THE OPERA

Released in December 1976, *A Day at the Races* was seen as a companion album to *A Night at the Opera*, continuing the Marx Brothers-themed titles and featuring a similar mix of styles. However, where *A Night at the Opera* had embraced an almost chaotic variety of genres and sounds, *A Day at the Races* presented a more cohesive and polished approach.

Freddie Mercury once again took center stage with tracks like "Somebody to Love," a gospel-inspired anthem that became one of the album's standout hits. Influenced by his love for Aretha Franklin and gospel music, Freddie wrote the song to showcase the band's vocal harmonies, layering their voices to create a full choir effect. The song's lyrics about loneliness and the search for love resonated deeply with listeners, and it quickly became one of Queen's most beloved songs.

Brian May's contributions to the album also stood out. Tracks like "Tie Your Mother Down" highlighted his ability to write riff-driven, hard-rocking anthems, while "Long Away" displayed his more reflective and melodic side. "Teo Torriatte (Let Us Cling Together)," one of May's most emotional pieces, was an ode to Queen's loyal Japanese fanbase and featured verses sung in Japanese—a testament to the band's growing international appeal.

The album's production was once again lavish, filled with multi-layered vocals, lush orchestration, and intricate guitar arrangements. However, the overall tone of *A Day at the Races* was more somber and introspective than its predecessor. Tracks like "You Take My Breath Away" and "The Millionaire Waltz" leaned into Freddie Mercury's love of ballads and classical music, showing a more intimate and reflective side of the band.

While *A Day at the Races* didn't achieve the same groundbreaking status as *A Night at the Opera*, it was still a commercial success, reaching number one in the UK and number five in the US. The album further solidified Queen's reputation as a band unafraid to experiment and explore new musical territories.

NEWS OF THE WORLD (1977): A SHIFT TOWARDS SIMPLICITY

As the band continued to evolve, they recognized that they couldn't repeat the formula of their last two albums indefinitely. In 1977, Queen shifted gears with the release of *News of the World*, an album that marked a significant departure from the complex, multi-layered arrangements of their previous work. The band wanted to strip down their sound and reconnect with the raw energy of rock music, in part as a response to the rise of punk rock.

Punk bands like The Sex Pistols and The Clash were challenging the established rock stars of the 1970s, and Queen—though vastly different in style—were paying attention. While they weren't about to embrace punk's minimalist ethos fully, they recognized that the time was right for a simpler, more direct approach to songwriting.

The result was *News of the World*, an album that opened with two of the most iconic anthems in rock history: "We Will Rock You" and "We Are the Champions." Written by Brian May and Freddie Mercury, respectively, these two tracks were designed with live performances in mind, and they quickly became staples of Queen's concerts. "We Will Rock You" featured May's now-legendary stomping rhythm and handclaps, creating a stadium-rock atmosphere that audiences couldn't resist. Meanwhile, "We Are the Champions," with its triumphant lyrics and soaring melody, became an anthem of victory and resilience.

The simplicity of these two songs contrasted with the more intricate compositions of earlier albums, but their impact was undeniable. They became massive hits, with "We Are the Champions" reaching the top 10 in the US and UK, and "We Will Rock You" cementing its place as a cultural phenomenon.

News of the World also featured other standout tracks like "Spread Your Wings," a power ballad written by John Deacon that showcased his growing confidence as a songwriter, and "Sheer Heart Attack," a fast-paced, punk-influenced track penned by Roger Taylor that directly responded to the rise of punk rock.

Despite the shift toward simplicity, Queen's trademark diversity was still present on *News of the World*. Tracks like "All Dead, All Dead" and "It's Late" featured Brian May's intricate guitar work, while Freddie Mercury's "My Melancholy Blues" offered a jazzy, introspective closing to the album. The balance of simplicity and complexity on *News of the World* proved that Queen could adapt to changing musical trends without losing their distinctive sound.

JAZZ (1978): A RETURN TO EXTRAVAGANCE

After the stripped-down sound of *News of the World*, Queen returned to a more extravagant approach with 1978's *Jazz*. True to its name, *Jazz* was an eclectic mix of styles, incorporating elements of funk, disco, hard rock, and even Middle Eastern influences. The album showcased Queen's refusal to be confined to a single genre, and its diversity both puzzled and delighted fans.

The album's lead single, "Fat Bottomed Girls," was a rollicking, tongue-in-cheek anthem penned by Brian May. It was paired with Freddie Mercury's disco-infused track "Bicycle Race," in a double A-side release that epitomized Queen's ability to blend humor and musicianship. The lyrics of "Bicycle Race," which were inspired by the Tour de France, reflected Freddie's playful and often surreal sense of humor.

Jazz also featured some of the band's more experimental songs. "Mustapha," written by Freddie Mercury, opened the album with a fusion of Middle Eastern melodies and rock, with Freddie singing in a mixture of English, Arabic, and nonsense words. The track was a bold statement that Queen wasn't afraid to venture into new musical territories, even at the risk of alienating some fans.

However, it was "Don't Stop Me Now" that became one of the album's most enduring hits. Written by Freddie Mercury, the song was a celebration of hedonism and freedom, with its upbeat tempo and infectious energy making it a fan favorite. Though it wasn't a massive hit upon its initial release, "Don't Stop Me Now" would later become one of Queen's most popular songs, thanks to its use in films, commercials, and television shows.

While *Jazz* wasn't as critically acclaimed as some of their earlier work, it was still a commercial success, reaching number 6 in the UK and number 6 in the US. The album's mix of styles and its return to a more flamboyant, over-the-top sound reinforced Queen's reputation as a band that thrived on diversity and unpredictability.

TOURING AND EXPANDING THEIR GLOBAL REACH

Throughout the late 1970s, Queen's sound continued to evolve, not just in the studio but on the road. Their live performances became increasingly elaborate, with larger venues and more ambitious stage designs. Freddie Mercury's stage presence grew even more dynamic, and the band's concerts became legendary for their energy and theatricality.

In 1977 and 1978, Queen embarked on extensive world tours, visiting countries they had never played in before, including Latin America and Asia. These tours helped solidify their status as one of the biggest live acts in the world. In South America, Queen became the first major rock band to play in several countries, performing to huge crowds in Argentina and Brazil. These shows not only boosted their global popularity but also demonstrated their ability to connect with audiences across cultural and language barriers.

Freddie Mercury's ability to command the stage and interact with fans, regardless of the language spoken, was key to Queen's international success. His flamboyant costumes, boundless energy, and powerful voice made every concert feel like an event, and fans around the world were drawn to his magnetic personality. Queen's live performances were more than just concerts—they were spectacles.

CONTINUING TO EVOLVE

As the 1970s drew to a close, Queen had evolved from a band with theatrical, experimental roots to a global rock phenomenon. Their ability to blend various genres, embrace new trends, and adapt to changing musical landscapes ensured that they remained relevant while staying true to their unique identity.

Despite critical ups and downs, Queen never shied away from taking risks, whether it was embracing punk's raw energy on *News of the World* or exploring disco and funk influences on *Jazz*. Their versatility, combined with Freddie Mercury's theatricality and Brian May's distinctive guitar work, ensured that Queen remained one of the most innovative and exciting bands of the era.

As they prepared to enter the 1980s, Queen stood at the peak of their powers, poised to conquer even greater heights with a new sound and a new era of music.

Chapter 5:
Freddie Mercury:
A Star's Persona

THE EARLY SIGNS OF STARDOM

Freddie Mercury, born Farrokh Bulsara, was already showing signs of star potential even before joining Queen. From his early days performing with bands in London to his flamboyant art school style, Freddie had an innate flair for drama and theatrics. But it wasn't until he found his place as the frontman of Queen that these qualities would flourish into the full-blown stage persona that captivated millions worldwide.

His transformation into "Freddie Mercury" was a deliberate and powerful move. Dropping his birth name and adopting the surname "Mercury" symbolized his larger-than-life ambitions. Freddie saw himself not merely as a singer, but as a performer—someone who would go beyond the music and embody the grandeur and drama of a rock star. The name Mercury was taken from the Roman god of communication and messages, fitting for someone who would become a commanding presence in both sound and spectacle.

Freddie's early years with Queen were marked by experimentation, both musically and visually. As the band began to climb the ranks of the British rock scene, Freddie's stage persona began to evolve. In the early 1970s, he wore flowing satin costumes and accessorized with feather boas and glitter, influenced by the glam rock movement popularized by artists like David Bowie and Marc Bolan. But even in these early days, it was clear that Freddie's charisma and energy set him apart from his contemporaries.

THE BIRTH OF THE SUPERSTAR FRONTMAN

By the mid-1970s, Freddie Mercury had fully embraced his role as the quintessential rock frontman. His stage presence was unparalleled—he wasn't just performing the songs; he was living them, turning every concert into a theatrical experience. Freddie had an uncanny ability to draw in his audience, making every person in the crowd feel like they were part of something extraordinary. Whether playing to a small club or a massive stadium, Freddie's charisma made even the largest venues feel intimate.

One of the defining features of Freddie's persona was his confidence. He carried himself with a regal air on stage, projecting an aura of control and authority. Whether in front of a microphone or a grand piano, Freddie commanded attention. His flamboyant outfits—ranging from skin tight sequined leotards to flowing capes and crowns—only amplified this persona. He wasn't just playing a part; he *was* the part.

Freddie's ability to engage with the audience was one of his greatest strengths. He could interact with a crowd of thousands as if they were his closest friends. Whether bantering between songs, gesturing dramatically with his microphone stand, or encouraging the audience to clap along, Freddie had a unique way of breaking down the barriers between performer and audience. This connection was particularly evident during songs like "We Will Rock You" and "We Are the Champions," which became communal anthems, with the entire crowd singing along as one.

VOCAL RANGE AND MUSICAL TALENT

As much as Freddie Mercury was known for his flamboyant stage presence, his vocal abilities were equally impressive. His voice was one of the most versatile and powerful in rock music, spanning nearly four octaves. Freddie could move effortlessly between a deep, rich baritone and a soaring tenor, all while maintaining incredible control and emotional depth.

Freddie's vocal range allowed him to experiment with different genres and musical styles, from the operatic highs of "Bohemian Rhapsody" to the soulful balladry of "Somebody to Love." His voice could be soft and tender, as heard in tracks like "Love of My Life," or raw and aggressive, as displayed in "Stone Cold Crazy." This versatility set him apart from many of his contemporaries and enabled Queen to explore a wide variety of musical landscapes without being confined to a single genre.

Beyond his vocals, Freddie was a talented pianist and songwriter. He wrote some of Queen's most iconic songs, including "Bohemian Rhapsody," "We Are the Champions," and "Somebody to Love." His ability to blend classical music with rock, pop, and even opera was key to Queen's innovative sound. His piano playing, often elegant and emotive, added a classical dimension to Queen's music that elevated their songs above the typical rock fare of the time.

ICONIC STAGE MOMENTS

Freddie Mercury's stage presence was defined by several key elements: his theatricality, his physicality, and his ability to create unforgettable moments. One of his signature stage moves was using his microphone stand as a prop. Early in his career, the stand accidentally broke, leaving him with only the top half. Instead of replacing it, Freddie incorporated the shortened mic stand into his performances, using it as a kind of baton to punctuate his gestures and movements. This would become one of his defining trademarks on stage.

As Queen's popularity grew, Freddie's stage antics became more daring and extravagant. He would strut across the stage with a combination of grace and swagger, his movements choreographed to match the drama of the music. In performances like "Bohemian Rhapsody," he would alternate between playing the piano and standing center stage, delivering powerful vocal lines that could send chills through an audience.

One of Freddie's most iconic stage moments came during Queen's performance at Live Aid in 1985. Broadcast to an estimated 1.9 billion people worldwide, the 20-minute set became one of the defining moments of Queen's career. Freddie, dressed simply in a white tank top and jeans, commanded the massive crowd at Wembley Stadium with ease. His call-and-response interaction with the audience, where he playfully vocalized and the crowd mimicked him, became a legendary moment, showcasing his ability to unite a stadium full of people with his voice alone.

This performance, often hailed as one of the greatest live rock performances in history, demonstrated the full extent of Freddie's stagecraft. He could switch from playful banter with the crowd to delivering soaring, emotional vocal performances in a matter of seconds. The energy and charisma Freddie exuded during this performance cemented his status as one of the greatest frontmen of all time.

THE PUBLIC VS. PRIVATE FREDDIE

While Freddie Mercury's public persona was one of exuberance, confidence, and flamboyance, his private life was far more complex and reserved. Off stage, Freddie was known to be shy and introspective. He famously valued his privacy, keeping much of his personal life out of the public eye. This contrast between his on-stage and off-stage personas only added to the mystique surrounding him.

Freddie had close relationships with a small circle of friends, including Mary Austin, his long-time confidante and former lover. He once described Mary as "the love of his life," and their bond remained strong even after they ended their romantic relationship. Despite being one of the most famous rock stars in the world, Freddie often sought solace in his private life, finding comfort in the company of those closest to him.

Freddie's sexuality was often a subject of speculation, particularly in the more conservative media climate of the 1970s and 1980s. While Freddie never publicly labeled his sexuality, he was open about his relationships with men in his private life. In interviews, he often deflected questions about his personal life with humour or ambiguous answers, preferring to keep the focus on his music rather than his personal affairs.

Freddie's private life became the subject of intense media scrutiny, especially in the years leading up to his battle with HIV/AIDS. Despite the tabloid rumours and speculation, Freddie remained intensely private about his illness, only making a public statement about his condition the day before his death in 1991. In his final years, Freddie continued to work and create music, even as his health deteriorated, demonstrating his dedication to his art.

INFLUENCE ON FUTURE GENERATIONS

Freddie Mercury's impact on the world of music and popular culture is immeasurable. His vocal prowess, flamboyant stage presence, and boundary-pushing creativity have inspired countless artists across a wide range of genres. Singers like Lady Gaga, Adam Lambert, and Brendon Urie have cited Freddie as a major influence, particularly for his ability to blend theatrics with musical integrity.

Freddie's openness about his sexuality, while not always publicized during his lifetime, has also made him a trailblazer for LGBTQ+ visibility in rock music. His unapologetic embrace of who he was, both as a performer and as an individual, has had a lasting impact on the LGBTQ+ community. His willingness to defy norms and expectations—both musically and personally—paved the way for future generations of artists to embrace their true selves without fear.

In addition to his influence on musicians, Freddie Mercury's larger-than-life persona has permeated popular culture. His image—whether in his iconic Live Aid outfit, his royal-inspired costumes, or his trademark mustache—remains instantly recognizable. Freddie's legacy as a performer, songwriter, and icon has only grown stronger since his passing, with his influence continuing to inspire new generations of fans and artists alike.

Chapter 6:
The 1980s: Global Domination and Change

THE SUCCESS OF THE GAME (1980)

As the 1980s began, Queen entered a new phase in their career with the release of *The Game*. Released in June 1980, this album marked a significant departure from the theatrical and eclectic style of their 1970s work, featuring a more streamlined and contemporary sound. The band had already shown their willingness to evolve musically, but *The Game* represented a deliberate effort to embrace new genres, including funk and disco, which were gaining mainstream popularity at the time.

One of the defining moments of *The Game* was the use of synthesizers. Up until this point, Queen had famously avoided synthesizers, proudly displaying the message "No Synths!" on their albums. But by 1980, they began to explore new sonic landscapes, using synths to add texture and depth to their songs. Tracks like "Play the Game" and "Save Me" blended traditional rock elements with the new possibilities offered by synthesizers, creating a fresh and contemporary sound that appealed to both rock fans and mainstream audiences.

The album's most significant single, "Another One Bites the Dust," was a major departure for Queen, fully embracing a funk-inspired groove. Written by John Deacon, the song was driven by a hypnotic bassline and minimalistic instrumentation, breaking away from the elaborate arrangements that had defined much of Queen's earlier work. "Another One Bites the Dust" became one of the band's biggest hits, reaching number one on the Billboard Hot 100 in the United States and charting highly in numerous other countries.

The success of "Another One Bites the Dust" was largely attributed to its crossover appeal. It was embraced by rock fans, disco lovers, and even hip-hop artists, who would later sample the track. The song's infectious rhythm and simple, repetitive lyrics made it a favourite on the dance floor, propelling Queen to new levels of global popularity.

The Game also featured the hit single "Crazy Little Thing Called Love," a rockabilly-inspired track that Freddie Mercury wrote in a matter of minutes while lounging in a bathtub. With its throwback sound and Elvis Presley-inspired vocals, the song was an instant hit, reaching number one in both the UK and the US. "Crazy Little Thing Called Love" showcased Queen's versatility, proving they could effortlessly shift between genres and still deliver chart-topping hits.

The Game became Queen's first album to reach number one in the United States, solidifying their position as a global rock powerhouse. The album's success marked the beginning of the band's domination of the early 1980s, as they embarked on a series of successful tours and continued to break new ground musically.

THE TRANSITION TO THE 1980S: EMBRACING NEW TRENDS

As the 1980s progressed, Queen's sound continued to evolve in response to changing musical trends. The rise of MTV in 1981 dramatically altered the landscape of the music industry, and music videos became a crucial promotional tool. Queen, always a band with a strong visual sense, embraced this new medium with open arms.

The music video for "Radio Ga Ga," released in 1984, became one of Queen's most iconic videos, directed by David Mallet. It featured a futuristic, dystopian aesthetic, inspired by Fritz Lang's 1927 silent film *Metropolis*, and depicted the band in a technologically advanced world where radio had been replaced by television. The video's imagery resonated with the growing influence of technology on popular culture, and the song itself became an anthem for fans who felt nostalgia for the golden age of radio.

"Radio Ga Ga" was more than just a hit single—it was a reflection of Queen's adaptability. The song embraced elements of synth-pop, a genre that was dominating the charts in the early 1980s. Roger Taylor, who wrote the song, was inspired by his own thoughts about the decline of radio and the rise of television, as well as his children's reaction to new musical trends. The song's catchy, chant-like chorus became an instant hit with live audiences, and it climbed to number two on the UK Singles Chart.

Along with "Radio Ga Ga," Queen released other tracks that showed their willingness to embrace the trends of the 1980s. Songs like "Under Pressure," their 1981 collaboration with David Bowie, demonstrated the band's ability to blend their signature sound with new wave influences. "Under Pressure" became an international hit, topping the charts in the UK and gaining widespread critical acclaim. The song's powerful bassline, combined with Freddie Mercury's and David Bowie's contrasting vocal styles, created a tension that resonated with listeners, and it has since become one of Queen's most enduring songs.

FACING CRITICISM: THE HOT SPACE ERA

While Queen's willingness to experiment had often paid off, their decision to fully embrace disco and funk with 1982's *Hot Space* proved to be one of the most divisive moments in their career. The album, heavily influenced by the success of "Another One Bites the Dust," featured a more electronic, dance-oriented sound, particularly in tracks like "Body Language" and "Back Chat." The decision to move away from their rock roots alienated some fans, especially in the United States, where the rock audience was less receptive to the new direction.

Hot Space was seen by many critics and fans as a misstep, with some accusing the band of chasing trends rather than staying true to their signature sound. "Body Language," in particular, with its minimalistic electronic beats and sultry lyrics, was a stark departure from the grandiosity of their previous work. The song's sexually charged music video was also controversial, further alienating some of their traditional fanbase.

However, not all was lost during the *Hot Space* era. While the album was polarizing, it still produced hits like "Under Pressure," which remained a fan favorite, and "Las Palabras de Amor (The Words of Love)," a heartfelt ballad inspired by the band's experiences in Latin America. The song reached number 17 in the UK Singles Chart and showcased Freddie's ability to convey deep emotion through his performance.

Queen's experimentation during this period can be seen as both a risk and a reflection of their unrelenting desire to evolve. Even when faced with criticism, the band refused to remain stagnant, continually exploring new sounds and pushing the boundaries of what rock music could be.

LIVE AID: QUEEN'S DEFINING MOMENT

Despite the challenges of the early 1980s, Queen's fortunes shifted dramatically in 1985 with their performance at the Live Aid charity concert. Organized by Bob Geldof and Midge Ure to raise funds for famine relief in Ethiopia, Live Aid was one of the largest music events in history, broadcast to over a billion people worldwide. Queen's 20-minute set at Wembley Stadium on July 13, 1985, became one of the most iconic live performances in rock history.

The band, who had been added to the lineup at the last minute, delivered a flawless performance that captivated both the live audience and viewers around the globe. Starting with "Bohemian Rhapsody" and ending with "We Are the Champions," Queen's set was a masterclass in showmanship. Freddie Mercury's interaction with the audience, particularly during the famous call-and-response section, where he improvised vocal lines and the crowd mimicked him, became the stuff of legend.

The performance at Live Aid revitalized Queen's career, especially in the United States, where their popularity had waned following the release of *Hot Space*. In the years following Live Aid, the performance was widely regarded as one of the greatest rock performances of all time, demonstrating Queen's ability to command a stage and connect with an audience on a massive scale.

For Freddie Mercury, Live Aid represented a personal triumph. In the years leading up to the event, there had been media speculation about his health and the future of the band, but his performance at Live Aid silenced those rumors. His powerful voice and magnetic stage presence reminded the world that Queen was still a force to be reckoned with, and it solidified Freddie's legacy as one of the greatest frontmen in rock history.

THE LATER YEARS OF THE DECADE: A KIND OF MAGIC AND BEYOND

Following the success of Live Aid, Queen entered a creative resurgence. In 1986, they released *A Kind of Magic*, an album that was heavily tied to the soundtrack of the film *Highlander*. The title track, "A Kind of Magic," became a major hit, reaching number three on the UK Singles Chart. The album also featured the song "Who Wants to Live Forever," written by Brian May, which became one of Queen's most haunting ballads, dealing with themes of mortality and love.

"A Kind of Magic* was well-received and marked a return to form after the mixed reactions to Hot Space. The album's accompanying tour, the Magic Tour, was a massive success, with Queen performing to sold-out stadiums across Europe. The tour included the now-legendary shows at Wembley Stadium, where the band played two nights to over 150,000 fans. These concerts were captured in the live album Live at Wembley '86, which showcased Queen at the peak of their live powers".

Tragically, the *Magic Tour* would be the last time Freddie Mercury would tour with Queen. As the 1980s progressed, Freddie's health began to decline, although the band continued to record music. In 1989, they released *The Miracle*, an album that hinted at the struggles Freddie was facing, with tracks like "The Miracle" and "Was It All Worth It" reflecting a more introspective and reflective tone.

QUEEN'S PLACE IN THE 1980S

By the end of the 1980s, Queen had successfully navigated the challenges of the decade, emerging stronger and more beloved than ever. Their ability to adapt to changing musical landscapes, from funk and disco to synth-pop, ensured their continued relevance in a rapidly evolving industry. Freddie

Mercury's larger-than-life persona, coupled with the band's musical versatility, helped Queen remain at the forefront of popular culture.

The 1980s were a decade of transformation for Queen. They experienced some of their greatest successes, including *The Game* and their performance at Live Aid, but they also faced significant challenges, including the divisive reception of *Hot Space* and the growing concerns about Freddie's health. Yet through it all, Queen's commitment to innovation, their unbreakable bond as a band, and their connection to their fans carried them forward.

As they looked toward the 1990s, Queen's legacy was already firmly established, and their influence on the world of music and performance was undeniable.

Chapter 7:
Live Aid: The Performance That Defined an Era

THE ROAD TO LIVE AID

By the mid-1980s, Queen had experienced both incredible success and some of the biggest challenges of their career. The success of albums like *The Game* had positioned them as one of the world's most popular rock bands, but their disco-influenced album *Hot Space* had alienated some fans, especially in the United States. At the same time, Queen's touring schedule was grueling, and there were growing tensions within the band. Freddie Mercury, in particular, was dealing with rumors about his personal life and health, and the band's future seemed uncertain.

Then came Live Aid. Organized by Bob Geldof and Midge Ure, the global charity concert aimed to raise funds for famine relief in Ethiopia. Taking place simultaneously at Wembley Stadium in London and John F. Kennedy Stadium in Philadelphia on July 13, 1985, the concert featured some of the biggest names in music, including U2, Elton John, David Bowie, The Who, and Paul McCartney.

At first, Queen wasn't certain whether they should participate. The band had taken a brief hiatus from touring after the release of *The Works* in 1984, and they weren't sure how they would fit into such a high-profile event, especially given their recent challenges in the United States. However, when they decided to take part, they knew they had to make it count. Freddie Mercury, in particular, was determined to put on the show of a lifetime.

PREPARING FOR THE SET

Queen's setlist for Live Aid was carefully crafted to ensure maximum impact. Unlike other bands who performed lengthy individual songs, Queen decided to pack as many of their biggest hits into the 20-minute time slot as possible. They chose songs that would get the crowd on their feet and involve the audience, songs that Freddie Mercury could use to engage the massive crowd at Wembley Stadium.

The band rehearsed intensely for the performance, refining their setlist down to six songs: "Bohemian Rhapsody," "Radio Ga Ga," "Hammer to Fall," "Crazy Little Thing Called Love," "We Will Rock You," and "We Are the Champions." Each of these tracks had been a massive hit, and each one was carefully chosen to showcase the band's versatility and power. They also shortened several songs to fit within the time constraints, ensuring there wouldn't be a single wasted moment on stage.

Freddie Mercury, despite growing speculation about his health, was in top form. He knew that this performance was a chance to remind the world of Queen's greatness, and he approached the event with his characteristic energy and determination. His voice, stage presence, and connection with the audience would prove to be the driving force behind what would become one of the greatest live performances in rock history.

QUEEN'S LIVE AID PERFORMANCE: A MASTERCLASS IN SHOWMANSHIP

At 6:41 PM on July 13, 1985, Queen took the stage at Wembley Stadium. From the moment Freddie Mercury sat at the piano and played the opening notes of "Bohemian Rhapsody," it was clear that something special was happening. The massive crowd of 72,000 erupted into cheers, and the world watched in awe as Queen delivered a performance that was nothing short of spectacular.

Freddie Mercury's command of the stage was undeniable. Dressed in a simple white tank top and jeans, with his signature mustache, Freddie captivated the audience with his charisma, energy, and vocal power. Despite the enormous scale of the event, Freddie had an almost magical ability to make the performance feel intimate, as if he were singing directly to each member of the crowd.

"Bohemian Rhapsody," with its operatic grandeur, was the perfect opener. The band seamlessly transitioned from the piano ballad section into the hard rock finale, with Brian May's soaring guitar solo filling the stadium. The audience, already familiar with the song's complex structure, sang along enthusiastically, fully immersed in the experience.

As the band moved into "Radio Ga Ga," the energy in the stadium only grew. The song's repetitive, chant-like chorus—"All we hear is Radio Ga Ga"—gave Freddie the perfect opportunity to engage with the audience, and they responded by clapping in unison, a visual and auditory spectacle that became one of the defining moments of the entire concert.

Next came "Hammer to Fall," a harder-edged rock song that demonstrated Queen's ability to shift between styles with ease. Brian May's powerful guitar riffs and Roger Taylor's driving drums energized the crowd, while Freddie Mercury strutted across the stage with his signature microphone stand, delivering a raw, electrifying vocal performance.

After "Crazy Little Thing Called Love," the band transitioned into their final two anthems, "We Will Rock You" and "We Are the Champions." By this point, the entire stadium was singing along, fully under Freddie's spell. The thundering stomp-clap rhythm of "We Will Rock You" shook the stadium, and as "We Are the Champions" reached its triumphant finale, it felt as if Queen had single-handedly united the entire world in a moment of pure musical magic.

FREDDIE MERCURY'S CALL-AND-RESPONSE: A LEGENDARY MOMENT

One of the most iconic moments of Queen's Live Aid set came during a brief but unforgettable call-and-response section between Freddie Mercury and the audience. Freddie, always the master showman, began improvising vocal runs, which the audience mimicked with perfect timing. "Ee-oh!" Freddie would sing, and the crowd would echo him with growing enthusiasm.

This moment, though spontaneous, highlighted Freddie's incredible ability to connect with a crowd. In those few minutes, Freddie held the entire stadium—and the millions watching at home—completely in his grasp. It wasn't just a performance; it was an interaction, a shared experience that transcended the usual boundaries of a live concert. Freddie's ability to improvise and engage with the audience in such a direct way became one of the most talked-about moments of Live Aid, and it has since gone down in history as one of the greatest moments in live performance.

THE AFTERMATH: QUEEN'S LEGACY REINVIGORATED

Queen's performance at Live Aid was a turning point for the band. While they had never been out of the spotlight, their popularity in the United States had waned in the early 1980s, especially after the mixed reception of *Hot Space*. Live Aid changed that. Almost overnight, Queen was once again seen as one of the greatest rock bands in the world, and their Live Aid set was hailed as the highlight of the entire event.

Critics who had once doubted the band's direction were now praising their performance, and fans who had drifted away returned in droves. The concert brought a renewed sense of purpose to Queen, and the band members—particularly Freddie Mercury—were reinvigorated by the experience.

In the months and years following Live Aid, the performance took on an almost mythical status. It was replayed countless times on television, discussed in the media, and lauded as one of the greatest live rock performances of all time. Even today, decades later, Queen's Live Aid set is regarded as a defining moment not only for the band but for live music in general.

FREDDIE MERCURY'S TRIUMPH

For Freddie Mercury, Live Aid was more than just a performance—it was a personal triumph. The press had been speculating about his health for months, and rumors about his personal life had begun to overshadow his musical contributions. But on July 13, 1985, none of that mattered. Freddie was at his absolute best, delivering a performance that silenced the critics and reaffirmed his place as one of the greatest frontmen in rock history.

Freddie's voice was as powerful as ever, hitting every note with precision and passion. His stage presence was magnetic, and his ability to connect with the audience—both in the stadium and watching at home—was unparalleled. For 20 minutes, Freddie Mercury owned the stage, and in doing so, he created a moment that would be remembered for generations.

LIVE AID'S IMPACT ON QUEEN'S CAREER

In the wake of Live Aid, Queen's career saw a resurgence. The band released *A Kind of Magic* in 1986, an album that served as the soundtrack for the film *Highlander*, and it became a major hit, especially in Europe. The album's success led to the *Magic Tour*, one of Queen's most successful tours, culminating in two sold-out shows at Wembley Stadium in 1986.

The energy from Live Aid carried Queen into the next phase of their career, with fans and critics alike celebrating the band's return to the top of the rock world. For Freddie Mercury, however, the triumph of Live Aid also marked the beginning of his final chapter. Though he continued to perform and record with Queen, his health would begin to decline in the years following the concert, and Live Aid would stand as one of his last truly great live performances.

LIVE AID'S LEGACY

Queen's performance at Live Aid remains one of the most celebrated moments in rock history. It wasn't just a great performance—it was a moment that captured the essence of live music at its best: spontaneous, emotional, and transcendent. It showcased Freddie Mercury's genius as a performer and reaffirmed Queen's place among the greatest bands of all time.

Live Aid itself raised millions of pounds for famine relief in Ethiopia, but it was Queen's performance that became the enduring symbol of the event. In the decades since, Live Aid has been viewed as a high point in Queen's career, and Freddie Mercury's legacy as one of rock's greatest frontmen was forever solidified.

Chapter 8:
Freddie Mercury's Solo Work

THE DESIRE FOR CREATIVE FREEDOM

By the early 1980s, Freddie Mercury had established himself as one of rock's most dynamic frontmen, yet his ambitions extended beyond Queen. While Queen's music allowed him to experiment with a wide range of genres, Freddie had a desire to explore his personal artistic identity even further. He wanted to venture into musical styles that were outside of Queen's typical repertoire, and so, in the mid-1980s, Freddie began working on solo projects.

Freddie's decision to pursue a solo career wasn't driven by any friction within Queen. In fact, the band remained intact throughout his solo endeavors. Freddie had always been an incredibly prolific songwriter, and his solo work gave him the opportunity to stretch his creative wings and explore more personal themes and styles. He saw his solo career as a complement to his work with Queen, rather than a replacement for it.

At the same time, the early 1980s was a period of transition for Freddie. The rise of disco, electronic music, and dance-pop had captured his interest, and he was eager to embrace these genres more fully. His flamboyant personality and love for dramatic, theatrical expression found a new outlet in his solo career, and he set out to create music that reflected his diverse interests.

MR. BAD GUY (1985): FREDDIE'S FIRST SOLO ALBUM

Freddie Mercury's first solo album, *Mr. Bad Guy*, was released in 1985, a few months before Queen's legendary Live Aid performance. The album represented a major departure from Queen's signature rock sound, featuring a mix of dance-pop, disco, and electronic music. While Freddie had experimented with these genres within Queen—particularly on *Hot Space*—*Mr. Bad Guy* gave him the freedom to fully immerse himself in these styles.

Freddie was deeply involved in the production of the album, taking on the role of both singer and producer. The title track, "Mr. Bad Guy," was a self-referential exploration of Freddie's public persona versus his private self. The song, with its playful lyrics and upbeat rhythm, showcased Freddie's ability to mix humor with introspection. Tracks like "Made in Heaven" and "Living on My Own" reflected Freddie's personal philosophy and longing for freedom, both musically and personally.

"Living on My Own," in particular, became one of the standout tracks on the album. Its infectious disco beat and celebratory lyrics reflected Freddie's love of nightlife and his desire for independence. However, it wasn't an instant hit. While the song later gained massive popularity after being remixed and re-released in 1993 (becoming a chart-topping hit in the UK), it initially flew under the radar.

Mr. Bad Guy was received with mixed reviews. Some critics praised Freddie's willingness to embrace pop and dance music, while others felt the album lacked the depth and complexity of his work with Queen. Commercially, it didn't achieve the success Freddie had hoped for. While it charted moderately well in the UK, reaching number six, it struggled in the United States.

Despite the album's modest success, *Mr. Bad Guy* allowed Freddie to explore new creative avenues and express aspects of his personality that weren't always at the forefront in Queen. He embraced his flamboyant, campy side more openly, celebrating life, love, and freedom. The album remains an important chapter in Freddie's artistic journey, reflecting both his desire for independence and his unapologetic embrace of who he was.

THE CHALLENGES OF GOING SOLO

Freddie's solo career was not without its challenges. While he enjoyed the creative freedom that came with working independently, he also found the process more difficult than expected. In Queen, the band functioned as a unit, with each member contributing ideas, refining songs, and pushing each other to achieve their best. As a solo artist, Freddie missed that collaborative energy.

Freddie was also acutely aware of the high expectations that came with his solo work. As the frontman of one of the biggest rock bands in the world, there was immense pressure for his solo career to live up to Queen's success. When *Mr. Bad Guy* didn't perform as well as hoped, Freddie felt the sting of disappointment. He later admitted that while he enjoyed the creative control of his solo work, he missed the camaraderie and structure of Queen.

Despite the mixed reception of his solo efforts, Freddie never saw his solo work as a failure. He viewed it as an opportunity to experiment, explore new sounds, and express himself more personally. For Freddie, success wasn't just about chart positions—it was about creative fulfillment.

BARCELONA (1988): A UNIQUE COLLABORATION

While *Mr. Bad Guy* was a personal and introspective project, Freddie's next solo endeavor, *Barcelona*, was a bold and ambitious collaboration that showcased his love for opera and classical music. Released in 1988, *Barcelona* was a collaborative album between Freddie and the acclaimed Spanish opera singer Montserrat Caballé.

Freddie had long admired opera and had been captivated by Montserrat Caballé's voice. In 1986, he met her at an event in Barcelona, where the two immediately connected over their shared love of music. Freddie expressed his desire to collaborate with her, and to his delight, Montserrat agreed. Over the next two years, they worked together to create *Barcelona*, an album that fused rock, pop, and opera in a way that had never been done before.

The title track, "Barcelona," became the standout song from the album. It was an operatic duet between Freddie and Montserrat, blending Freddie's soaring vocals with Montserrat's powerful, classically trained voice. The song was a celebration of the city of Barcelona and was later chosen as the anthem for the 1992 Summer Olympics, which were held in the city. Freddie, always the showman, delivered a passionate performance, reveling in the chance to sing alongside one of his idols.

The rest of the album continued in the same vein, with tracks like "The Golden Boy" and "How Can I Go On" blending the dramatic, emotional intensity of opera with Freddie's distinctive pop sensibilities. While *Barcelona* was not a commercial blockbuster, it was a critical success and was praised for its daring and originality. For Freddie, it was a dream come true—he had always wanted to merge his love of rock and classical music, and *Barcelona* gave him the chance to do so on a grand scale.

Barcelona demonstrated Freddie's versatility as an artist. While many rock stars stuck to their established sound, Freddie fearlessly ventured into new territory, unafraid to take risks. The album remains a unique part of his legacy, showcasing his passion for music beyond the confines of rock and pop.

SOLO WORK AND QUEEN: COMPLEMENTARY WORLDS

Although Freddie's solo work allowed him to explore his individual artistic identity, it never took away from his commitment to Queen. In fact, Freddie's solo career seemed to enhance his work with the band, giving him new creative energy that he brought back to Queen's recordings. While some fans worried that Freddie's solo ventures might lead to a permanent break from Queen, Freddie made it clear that the band remained his priority.

The differences between Freddie's solo work and his work with Queen were stark. While his solo albums were more focused on dance, pop, and electronic music, his work with Queen was broader in scope, incorporating rock, opera, classical, and theatrical elements. Queen's music was more collaborative, with each member contributing to the overall sound, while Freddie's solo work was a more personal expression of his individual tastes.

Freddie's ability to balance both worlds—his flamboyant solo persona and his role as Queen's frontman—was a testament to his versatility as an artist. He thrived in both settings, whether he was performing a disco anthem like "Living on My Own" or leading Queen through a rock epic like "We Are the Champions."

FREDDIE'S LEGACY AS A SOLO ARTIST

Freddie Mercury's solo career may not have reached the commercial heights of his work with Queen, but it remains an essential part of his legacy. His willingness to take risks, explore new genres, and collaborate with artists from different musical backgrounds demonstrated his boundless creativity. Whether embracing pop, disco, or opera, Freddie was always pushing the boundaries of what was expected from a rock star.

Freddie's solo work also revealed a more personal side of his artistry. In songs like "Love Me Like There's No Tomorrow" and "Time," Freddie explored themes of love, longing, and mortality. These songs, often overlooked in favor of Queen's larger-than-life hits, provide a glimpse into Freddie's inner world and his reflections on life.

While his solo career may not have eclipsed Queen's monumental success, it allowed Freddie to experiment and express himself in ways that Queen's music didn't always allow. His work with Montserrat Caballé on *Barcelona* remains one of the most daring and unexpected collaborations in rock history, and it showcased Freddie's passion for opera and classical music.

As an artist, Freddie Mercury was never content to rest on his laurels. His solo career was a testament to his desire for growth, exploration, and self-expression. It complemented his work with Queen and added another dimension to his already legendary legacy.

Chapter 9:
Late 1980s: Struggles and Triumphs

THE RELEASE OF THE MIRACLE (1989)

By the late 1980s, Queen was facing both personal and professional challenges. Despite their continued popularity, there were growing concerns about Freddie Mercury's health, as rumors about his illness began to spread in the press. Yet, despite these obstacles, Queen remained creatively active and continued to produce music that resonated with fans around the world.

In May 1989, Queen released *The Miracle*, their thirteenth studio album. The album marked a return to form after the mixed reception of *Hot Space* and the success of *A Kind of Magic*. While the band had stopped touring after the *Magic Tour* in 1986, *The Miracle* demonstrated that Queen was still very much a force to be reckoned with in the studio.

The Miracle was a celebratory and uplifting album, despite the challenges the band was facing behind the scenes. It reflected their unity as a group and their commitment to continuing as a band, even as Freddie's health was becoming a growing concern. The album's themes of togetherness, resilience, and reflection were apparent in tracks like "The Miracle" and "Was It All Worth It," which explored both the triumphs and challenges of the band's career.

The title track, "The Miracle," was an optimistic and anthemic celebration of life's wonders. It was a declaration of unity, with the band members appearing together on the album cover as a composite image, symbolizing their solidarity and shared purpose. The song's message of hope and the miraculous nature of life resonated deeply with fans, particularly given the context of Freddie's illness, even though the band had not yet confirmed it publicly.

Other standout tracks from the album included "I Want It All," a hard-rock anthem written by Brian May that captured the band's defiant spirit, and "Breakthru," an energetic, upbeat track that showcased Queen's ability to blend rock with pop sensibilities. "I Want It All" became one of Queen's biggest hits of the late 1980s, reaching number three on the UK Singles Chart and resonating with fans who saw the song as a reflection of the band's resilience.

FREDDIE'S BATTLE WITH AIDS

Behind the scenes, however, Freddie Mercury was facing the most difficult battle of his life. Although he had not yet made his illness public, Freddie had been diagnosed with HIV in 1987. At the time, the disease carried a heavy stigma, and little was known about effective treatments. Freddie's diagnosis marked the beginning of a long and painful journey as he struggled to maintain his privacy while also continuing to work with Queen.

Freddie's decision to keep his illness private was driven by his desire to focus on his music rather than becoming a subject of media speculation. While the press had begun to circulate rumors about Freddie's health—fueled by his increasingly gaunt appearance—Freddie refused to confirm or deny the stories. He believed that his personal life was his own business, and he wanted to continue working as long as he was able.

Despite his declining health, Freddie remained incredibly dedicated to Queen and to his music. His work ethic was unparalleled, and he continued to record new material with the band even as his illness progressed. For Freddie, music was a form of solace, and he poured everything he had into the recording sessions for *The Miracle*. His determination to continue creating music, even in the face of such adversity, was a testament to his strength and passion as an artist.

THE BAND'S SHIFT TO STUDIO WORK

As Freddie's illness progressed, Queen made the collective decision to stop touring after 1986, focusing instead on studio work. This decision allowed Freddie to conserve his energy while still contributing to the band's creative output. The members of Queen were deeply protective of Freddie, respecting his need for privacy and supporting him throughout his battle with AIDS.

The shift to studio work allowed Queen to experiment more freely with production techniques and soundscapes. Without the pressure of preparing for live performances, the band could take their time in the studio, refining their songs and exploring new ideas. Brian May, Roger Taylor, and John Deacon all stepped up to contribute more to the songwriting process, while Freddie continued to lead with his vocals and creative vision.

While they were no longer touring, Queen remained connected with their fans through their music videos, which became increasingly important as a way to promote their albums. The video for "I Want It All," directed by David Mallet, became one of the defining images of Queen in the late 1980s. The video showcased the band performing in a minimalist setting, with Freddie commanding the screen despite his fragile health. Fans were struck by his energy and presence, even though it was clear that Freddie was no longer the vibrant performer he had once been.

THE MEDIA SPECULATION AND FREDDIE'S PRIVACY

As Freddie's illness progressed, media speculation about his health became increasingly intrusive. Tabloid newspapers published sensationalized stories about Freddie's condition, with many claiming that he was suffering from AIDS, even though the band continued to deny these reports. The media frenzy was relentless, with photographers camped outside Freddie's home and reporters hounding him for confirmation.

Freddie, ever the private individual, refused to engage with the press on the subject of his health. He believed that his illness was his own business and that his work should be judged on its own merits, rather than being overshadowed by speculation about his personal life. The other members of Queen supported

Freddie in this decision, remaining tight-lipped about his condition even as the rumors intensified.

The pressure from the media only strengthened Freddie's resolve to continue working. Despite the physical toll that AIDS was taking on his body, he was determined to keep recording with Queen for as long as possible. In the face of immense personal suffering, Freddie continued to deliver powerful vocal performances, demonstrating his unwavering commitment to his music and his legacy.

THE EMOTIONAL WEIGHT OF THE MIRACLE

Though *The Miracle* was, on the surface, an uplifting and celebratory album, it also carried emotional weight, particularly in hindsight. Songs like "Was It All Worth It" hinted at a more introspective and reflective tone, with Freddie contemplating the highs and lows of his life and career. The song's lyrics, which ponder the meaning of fame and the sacrifices that come with it, were especially poignant given Freddie's ongoing battle with AIDS.

Freddie's performances on *The Miracle* were nothing short of remarkable. Despite the physical toll of his illness, his voice remained as powerful and dynamic as ever. He delivered each song with passion and conviction, as if aware that his time was limited and determined to make the most of every moment he had left. Tracks like "Breakthru" and "The Miracle" reflected Freddie's optimism and desire to live life to the fullest, while songs like "The Invisible Man" and "Scandal" revealed his frustration with the media's relentless pursuit of his private life.

The Miracle also reflected the unity of the band during this difficult time. The album was one of Queen's most collaborative efforts, with each member contributing to the songwriting and production. It was clear that the band had rallied around Freddie, supporting him both personally and professionally as they worked together to create music that would stand the test of time.

QUEEN'S CONTINUED POPULARITY

Despite the challenges they faced, Queen's popularity remained strong in the late 1980s. *The Miracle* was a commercial success, reaching number one in the UK and charting in several other countries. The album produced several hit singles, including "I Want It All," "Breakthru," and "The Invisible Man," each of which was accompanied by a visually striking music video that showcased the band's creativity and Freddie's indomitable spirit.

In addition to their success in the UK, Queen's international fanbase continued to grow, particularly in countries like Japan and Latin America, where their popularity had soared since the early 1980s. The band's decision to stop touring did little to diminish their appeal, and their music videos, televised performances, and album releases kept them in the public eye.

FACING AN UNCERTAIN FUTURE

As the 1980s drew to a close, Queen faced an uncertain future. Freddie's health continued to deteriorate, and the band was well aware that their time together was limited. Yet, despite these challenges, Queen remained committed to their music and to each other. The bond between the four members had never been stronger, and they approached their work with a sense of purpose and urgency, knowing that every recording session could be their last.

Freddie's decision to keep his illness private meant that the full extent of his suffering was not widely known, even to some of his closest friends. But within the band, there was a deep understanding of what was happening. Brian, Roger, and John were determined to support Freddie in any way they could, and their loyalty to him was unwavering.

Though the band's future was uncertain, their legacy was already secure. Queen had become one of the most successful and influential rock bands in history, with a body of work that spanned nearly two decades. As they prepared to enter the 1990s, they knew that their next album would likely be their last with Freddie—but they were determined to make it their best.

Chapter 10:
Innuendo and Freddie's Final Years

THE EMOTIONAL WEIGHT OF THE SONGS (CONTINUED)

"These Are the Days of Our Lives" became one of the most poignant tracks on *Innuendo*. Written by Roger Taylor, the song was a reflective look back on the simplicity and beauty of life, as well as an acknowledgment of its fleeting nature. The lyrics—"Those were the days of our lives / The bad things in life were so few / Those days are all gone now, but one thing's still true"—seemed to capture Freddie Mercury's acceptance of his situation. The accompanying music video, shot in black and white to soften Freddie's appearance as his illness progressed, features what would be Freddie's final on-camera performance with Queen.

In the video, Freddie, though visibly weakened, remains defiant and composed. His final gesture—a whispered "I still love you" directly to the camera—was a heartfelt message to his fans, leaving them with a sense of closeness despite the physical distance his illness created. The video became an enduring image of Freddie's final days, both vulnerable and powerful.

Another standout track, "The Show Must Go On," written primarily by Brian May, served as an anthem of resilience and perseverance. Despite his declining health, Freddie delivered one of his most powerful vocal performances, defying the physical limitations imposed by his illness. The lyrics—"Inside my heart is breaking / My make-up may be flaking / But my smile still stays on"—are a reflection of Freddie's unwavering spirit, a testament to his desire to continue creating music even as his body was failing him.

Brian May later revealed that when the band was preparing to record "The Show Must Go On," he wasn't sure if Freddie would be physically able to sing it. However, in true Freddie fashion, he took a shot of vodka, stood at the microphone, and delivered the performance in a single take. It was one of the most emotionally charged moments in the recording sessions, and it encapsulated Freddie's determination to live and create music until the very end.

FREDDIE'S LAST DAYS IN THE STUDIO

Throughout the recording of *Innuendo*, Freddie Mercury continued to push himself to the limit, working on music even as his illness progressed. His physical condition had deteriorated significantly by this point, but Freddie's passion for music remained undiminished. Brian May, Roger Taylor, and John Deacon were deeply affected by Freddie's bravery and dedication, and they supported him every step of the way.

Freddie was aware that *Innuendo* would likely be his final album with Queen, and this knowledge imbued the recording sessions with a sense of urgency and gravity. Though the band tried to maintain a sense of normalcy in the studio, there was an unspoken understanding that they were recording their last work with their beloved frontman.

Freddie's energy in the studio was nothing short of remarkable. Even as his illness left him bedridden for much of the day, he would muster the strength to record his vocals, often lying down in between takes to rest. Brian May later recounted how Freddie, even in his weakened state, refused to compromise on the quality of his performances. He insisted on delivering each song with the same passion and intensity that had defined his entire career.

In addition to *Innuendo*, the band also recorded several other tracks that would later appear on *Made in Heaven*, Queen's posthumous album released in 1995. These sessions were bittersweet, as the band knew that their time with Freddie was running out, yet they wanted to capture as much of his voice and spirit as possible while they still could.

FREDDIE'S PUBLIC STATEMENT

As Freddie's health continued to decline throughout 1991, media speculation about his condition intensified. Tabloid journalists camped outside his London home, desperate for confirmation of the rumors that had been circulating for years. Despite the pressure, Freddie had remained private about his battle with AIDS, choosing to focus on his work and his music rather than engage with the press.

However, on November 23, 1991, just one day before his death, Freddie Mercury made a public statement confirming what many had suspected: that he was living with AIDS. In the statement, Freddie wrote, "I felt it correct to keep this information private to protect the privacy of those around me. However, the time has come now for my friends and fans around the world to know the truth, and I hope everyone will join with me, my doctors, and all those worldwide in the fight against this terrible disease."

This public acknowledgment was both brave and tragic, as it came at a time when Freddie was nearing the end of his life. He had chosen to keep his illness private for as long as possible, focusing on the things he loved—his music, his friends, and his fans. But in his final act of courage, Freddie hoped to raise awareness about AIDS and to help fight the stigma that surrounded the disease.

FREDDIE'S DEATH AND THE WORLD'S REACTION

On November 24, 1991, just one day after his public statement, Freddie Mercury passed away at his home in Kensington, London, surrounded by close friends and loved ones, including his long-time friend and former partner Mary Austin. The official cause of death was bronchial pneumonia, a complication of AIDS.

The news of Freddie's death sent shockwaves around the world. Fans, many of whom had grown up with Queen's music, were devastated by the loss of one of rock's greatest icons. Tributes poured in from across the music industry, with artists, fellow musicians, and celebrities expressing their admiration for Freddie's talent and legacy. Elton John, David Bowie, and George Michael were among the many who paid tribute to Freddie, acknowledging the profound impact he had on their own careers and on the music industry as a whole.

In the days following Freddie's death, fans gathered outside his home, leaving flowers, notes, and messages of love and support. For many, Freddie was more than just a rock star—he was an inspiration, a symbol of defiance, and a figure who embraced his individuality and encouraged others to do the same. His death marked the end of an era for Queen, but it also solidified Freddie's status as a cultural icon whose influence would endure for generations.

INNUENDO AND FREDDIE'S LEGACY

Innuendo became one of Queen's most critically acclaimed albums, not just for its musical innovation but also for the emotional weight it carried as Freddie Mercury's final artistic statement. The album topped the charts in the UK and across Europe, and its success was a testament to Freddie's enduring appeal even as he faced his greatest personal challenges.

Tracks like "The Show Must Go On" and "These Are the Days of Our Lives" took on new meaning after Freddie's death, with fans and critics alike interpreting them as Freddie's farewell to the world. The emotional depth of these songs, combined with Freddie's powerful vocals, made *Innuendo* a fitting final chapter in Queen's career with Freddie at the helm.

Freddie Mercury's death was a profound loss to the world of music, but his legacy continued to grow in the years that followed. In 1992, a tribute concert was held at Wembley Stadium in his honor, featuring performances by some of the biggest names in music, including David Bowie, George Michael, and Elton John. The concert raised millions of pounds for AIDS awareness and research, continuing the fight that Freddie had sought to support in his final days.

Freddie's influence on music, fashion, and culture remained strong long after his passing. His flamboyant stage presence, fearless approach to life, and powerful vocal abilities inspired countless artists across multiple genres. His willingness to live authentically, both on and off stage, made him a trailblazer for LGBTQ+ representation in rock music.

THE SHOW MUST GO ON

Freddie Mercury's final years were marked by both immense personal struggle and artistic triumph. Even as his health declined, Freddie never lost his passion for music, and he continued to create until the very end. His work on *Innuendo* and the other songs recorded during this time stand as a testament to his enduring strength and creativity.

Freddie's final message, delivered through songs like "The Show Must Go On," was one of perseverance and hope. Though he may have left the world far too soon, Freddie's music, charisma, and spirit live on. For his millions of fans, Freddie's legacy is not just one of incredible music—it is a legacy of resilience, courage, and the unyielding belief that the show, indeed, must go on.

Chapter 11:
The Legacy Of Freddie Mercury

THE IMMEDIATE IMPACT OF FREDDIE'S DEATH

Freddie Mercury's death on November 24, 1991, marked a profound moment in music history. The world lost one of its most dynamic performers, and Queen lost its iconic frontman. In the days following his death, tributes poured in from across the globe, highlighting the deep admiration and love that people had for Freddie. The media, which had hounded him for years about his health and personal life, quickly shifted to celebrate his achievements as one of the greatest rock stars in history.

Freddie's death also brought much-needed attention to the AIDS epidemic, which was still heavily stigmatized in the early 1990s. Freddie's bravery in publicly acknowledging his illness just a day before his death helped shift the public perception of AIDS, and his death served as a rallying cry for greater awareness and funding for AIDS research. In the wake of Freddie's passing, his friends, fans, and fellow musicians came together to honor his legacy and to fight the disease that had claimed his life.

THE FREDDIE MERCURY TRIBUTE CONCERT

One of the most significant events following Freddie's death was the Freddie Mercury Tribute Concert for AIDS Awareness, held on April 20, 1992, at Wembley Stadium. The concert was organized by the surviving members of Queen—Brian May, Roger Taylor, and John Deacon—as a way to celebrate Freddie's life and raise money for AIDS research.

The concert featured an extraordinary lineup of some of the biggest names in music, all of whom had been influenced by Freddie and Queen. Performers included Elton John, David Bowie, Annie Lennox, George Michael, and Robert Plant, among many others. Each artist brought their own style to Queen's iconic songs, creating memorable collaborations that paid tribute to Freddie's incredible range and influence.

One of the standout moments of the night was George Michael's powerful rendition of "Somebody to Love," which has since become one of the most celebrated performances in tribute to Freddie. David Bowie's duet with Annie Lennox on "Under Pressure" and Elton John's performance of "The Show Must Go On" were also highlights, showcasing the emotional depth and universal appeal of Queen's music.

The concert was attended by over 72,000 people and was broadcast to an estimated audience of one billion worldwide, making it one of the largest televised music events in history. More importantly, the event raised millions of pounds for AIDS research and helped to destigmatize the disease, continuing the work that Freddie had quietly supported during his life.

THE MERCURY PHOENIX TRUST

In the aftermath of Freddie's death, the remaining members of Queen, along with Freddie's close friend and manager Jim Beach, founded the Mercury Phoenix Trust. The trust was established to honor Freddie's memory by raising money for AIDS awareness and education. Since its founding in 1992, the Mercury Phoenix Trust has raised millions of pounds for global HIV/AIDS initiatives, funding projects that focus on prevention, education, and care for those living with the disease.

The trust became one of the key legacies of Freddie's life, ensuring that his name would continue to be associated with the fight against AIDS. The trust's work has had a profound impact on communities around the world, particularly in areas where HIV/AIDS remains a significant health crisis. For Freddie's fans, the Mercury Phoenix Trust serves as a reminder of his generosity, compassion, and commitment to making the world a better place.

FREDDIE'S CULTURAL LEGACY

Freddie Mercury's impact on popular culture extends far beyond his contributions to music. He was a trailblazer in terms of self-expression, individuality, and creativity, and his influence can be seen in countless artists who followed in his footsteps. Freddie's bold stage presence, flamboyant fashion sense, and fearless embrace of his identity made him a cultural icon, and his legacy continues to inspire people across the world to be true to themselves.

Freddie's influence on LGBTQ+ culture is especially significant. As one of the first openly bisexual rock stars to achieve global fame, Freddie became a symbol of LGBTQ+ pride, even though he kept much of his personal life private during his lifetime. In the years since his death, Freddie has been embraced by the LGBTQ+ community as a figure of courage and authenticity. His flamboyant performances, unapologetic individuality, and boundary-pushing creativity helped pave the way for greater LGBTQ+ visibility in the music industry and beyond.

Freddie's music and image have continued to resonate with new generations of fans. His iconic look—from his glamorous 1970s persona to his later, more masculine image with his trademark mustache and short hair—remains instantly recognizable. His influence on fashion and style can still be seen in contemporary artists who embrace a mix of theatricality and gender-fluid expression.

QUEEN'S POST-FREDDIE CAREER

Following Freddie's death, the remaining members of Queen faced a difficult decision about the future of the band. Without Freddie, the idea of continuing Queen as it had existed seemed impossible. John Deacon, in particular, struggled with the loss of Freddie, and after contributing to Queen's final project, *Made in Heaven* (1995), he retired from the music industry.

Brian May and Roger Taylor, however, remained active in music and eventually decided to continue performing Queen's music, albeit in a different format. In the early 2000s, Queen began collaborating with Paul Rodgers, the former frontman of Free and Bad Company, for a series of tours. While Rodgers' bluesy rock style was a departure from Freddie's flamboyant theatrics, the collaboration allowed Queen's music to reach new audiences.

In 2011, Queen found a new frontman in Adam Lambert, a singer with an extraordinary vocal range and a flair for theatrical performance, much like Freddie. The collaboration, branded as Queen + Adam Lambert, brought Queen's music to a new generation of fans, with the band performing to sold-out arenas around the world. While Lambert has never tried to imitate Freddie, his performances have been praised for honoring Freddie's legacy while bringing his own unique style to Queen's timeless music.

BOHEMIAN RHAPSODY: THE FILM

Freddie Mercury's life and legacy were immortalized in the 2018 biographical film *Bohemian Rhapsody*, which chronicled Queen's rise to fame and Freddie's personal struggles, leading up to their legendary performance at Live Aid. Directed by Bryan Singer (and later Dexter Fletcher), the film starred Rami Malek as Freddie Mercury, a role that earned Malek an Academy Award for Best Actor.

The film was a massive box office success, grossing over $900 million worldwide, and it introduced Queen's music to a new generation of fans. Despite some criticism for historical inaccuracies and its handling of certain aspects of Freddie's personal life, *Bohemian Rhapsody* was widely praised for its celebration of Freddie's legacy and the emotional impact of its portrayal of his life.

The film also reignited interest in Queen's music, with Queen's songs once again topping charts around the world. For many younger fans, *Bohemian Rhapsody* served as their introduction to Queen's incredible body of work, ensuring that Freddie's influence would continue to grow well into the 21st century.

FREDDIE MERCURY'S INFLUENCE ON FUTURE GENERATIONS

Freddie Mercury's influence on music and culture has only grown since his death. Countless artists, from Lady Gaga and Adam Lambert to Brendon Urie and Harry Styles, have cited Freddie as a major influence on their careers. His ability to blend musical genres, his theatrical stage presence, and his unapologetic self-expression have inspired generations of musicians, performers, and creatives.

Freddie's vocal prowess, in particular, remains legendary. His ability to seamlessly transition between different vocal styles, from rock to opera to ballads, has set a benchmark for vocalists in the music industry. His range, power, and emotional depth have made him one of the most revered singers in rock history.

Beyond music, Freddie's legacy as a champion of individuality and self-expression has left an indelible mark on culture. He embodied the idea that it's okay to be different, to take risks, and to embrace who you are. His willingness to defy convention and live life on his own terms has made him a cultural icon for people of all backgrounds.

FREDDIE'S IMMORTALITY IN POPULAR CULTURE

Freddie Mercury's legacy has continued to thrive in popular culture. His image, music, and story have been immortalized in countless forms, from tribute albums and biographical films to books, documentaries, and stage productions. His signature songs—"Bohemian Rhapsody," "We Are the Champions," "Somebody to Love," and many others—have become anthems that transcend generations.

Freddie's larger-than-life persona continues to captivate new audiences, and his influence can be seen in the performances of modern-day artists who, like Freddie, push boundaries and celebrate individuality. Whether through Queen's music, the Mercury Phoenix Trust's ongoing fight against AIDS, or the countless tributes paid to him by fans and musicians alike, Freddie Mercury's legacy endures as a symbol of creativity, courage, and the power of music to unite and inspire.

Chapter 12:
Queen After Freddie:
A New Era

COPING WITH FREDDIE'S LOSS

Freddie Mercury's death in 1991 left a profound void in Queen, both personally and musically. For over two decades, Freddie had been the band's charismatic frontman, creative force, and close friend. His unique vocal abilities and larger-than-life stage presence were irreplaceable, and his passing left the remaining members—Brian May, Roger Taylor, and John Deacon—grappling with how to move forward.

In the immediate aftermath of Freddie's death, Queen took a step back from the spotlight. The band members were still processing their grief and unsure if they could, or even wanted to, continue without Freddie. John Deacon, in particular, found it difficult to carry on without Freddie. Deeply affected by the loss of his friend, Deacon gradually withdrew from the music industry, playing his last show with Queen in 1997 and retiring from public life soon after.

However, both Brian May and Roger Taylor remained committed to keeping Queen's legacy alive. In the years following Freddie's death, they faced the challenge of honoring Freddie's memory while also finding new ways to bring Queen's music to audiences. For May and Taylor, the question wasn't how to replace Freddie—that was impossible—but how to continue sharing the band's music with the world in a way that respected the band's past while looking toward the future.

MADE IN HEAVEN (1995): FREDDIE'S FINAL GIFT

In 1995, four years after Freddie's death, Queen released *Made in Heaven*, the last album to feature Freddie Mercury's voice. The album was a labor of love for the band, as it included vocal recordings Freddie had made during his final days, as well as material from earlier sessions that had not yet been completed.

Freddie had continued recording vocals for as long as his health allowed, knowing that the band would finish the tracks after his death. His dedication was remarkable, and he approached these sessions with the same passion and professionalism that had defined his entire career. As Brian May later recounted, Freddie would say, "I'll sing until I bloody well drop."

Made in Heaven was an emotional farewell, both for the band and for Queen's fans. Tracks like "A Winter's Tale" and "Mother Love" reflected a more introspective and tender side of Freddie, while songs like "Let Me Live" and "Too Much Love Will Kill You" carried a sense of longing and finality. The album was both a celebration of life and an acknowledgment of loss, as the remaining members of Queen worked tirelessly to honor Freddie's legacy.

The album was a commercial success, topping the charts in the UK and performing well in several other countries. For fans, *Made in Heaven* was a deeply personal and emotional experience, as they heard Freddie's voice one last time on new Queen material. The release of the album helped bring a sense of closure to the band's story with Freddie, but it also left fans wondering what the future held for Queen.

JOHN DEACON'S RETIREMENT

Following the release of *Made in Heaven*, John Deacon made the decision to step away from Queen and the music industry altogether. Deacon had always been the most private and reserved member of the band, and Freddie's death affected him deeply. He felt that without Freddie, Queen could not continue in the same way, and he struggled with the idea of performing Queen's music without their iconic frontman.

After performing at the 1997 charity concert in Paris, where he joined Brian May and Roger Taylor for a rendition of "The Show Must Go On" with Elton John, Deacon quietly retired from public life. While he has maintained a low profile since then, Deacon's contributions to Queen's legacy are undeniable. As the composer of some of Queen's biggest hits, including "Another One Bites the Dust," "I Want to Break Free," and "You're My Best Friend," his work continues to resonate with fans around the world.

Deacon's departure left Brian May and Roger Taylor as the remaining members of Queen, and while they respected John's decision, they were determined to continue sharing Queen's music with new generations of fans.

COLLABORATIONS WITH PAUL RODGERS (2004–2009)

In 2004, after years of various side projects and solo ventures, Brian May and Roger Taylor decided to revive Queen in a new form, collaborating with legendary rock vocalist Paul Rodgers. Rodgers, known for his work with Free and Bad Company, brought a bluesy, hard rock sensibility to Queen's music, and the new collaboration was branded as "Queen + Paul Rodgers."

While Rodgers' style was quite different from Freddie Mercury's, his powerful voice and stage presence allowed Queen's music to take on a fresh energy. The collaboration was well-received, particularly by fans who appreciated the band's willingness to move forward while honoring their past.

Queen + Paul Rodgers embarked on a series of successful tours, performing Queen classics alongside Rodgers' own hits from his time with Free and Bad Company. The partnership culminated in the release of an album, *The Cosmos Rocks*, in 2008, which featured original material written by May, Taylor, and Rodgers.

However, despite the success of the tours and the album, Queen + Paul Rodgers was never intended to be a permanent arrangement. After their final tour in 2009, Rodgers amicably parted ways with May and Taylor, and Queen once again found themselves at a crossroads.

QUEEN + ADAM LAMBERT: A NEW ERA BEGINS

In 2011, Queen found a new collaborator in Adam Lambert, a singer with a powerful vocal range and a theatrical stage presence that was often compared to Freddie Mercury's. Lambert had risen to fame as the runner-up on *American Idol*, where he performed Queen's "Bohemian Rhapsody" during his audition and later performed with May and Taylor during the show's finale.

The chemistry between Lambert and Queen was undeniable, and in 2012, they officially launched the "Queen + Adam Lambert" collaboration. Lambert's vocal abilities allowed him to perform Queen's iconic songs with respect and power, while his flamboyant stage presence paid tribute to Freddie without attempting to imitate him.

Queen + Adam Lambert embarked on several highly successful world tours, performing to sold-out arenas and introducing Queen's music to a new generation of fans. While the band's sound had evolved over the years, the heart of Queen—it's anthemic songs, its powerful performances, and its connection with audiences—remained intact.

Lambert's collaboration with Queen has been widely praised by both fans and critics. He has been lauded for his ability to honor Freddie's legacy while bringing his own unique style to the performances. Brian May and Roger Taylor, too, have expressed their gratitude for the partnership, which has allowed them to continue performing and sharing Queen's music with the world.

REVISITING QUEEN'S LEGACY

In the years following Freddie Mercury's death, Queen's legacy has only grown stronger. The band's music continues to be celebrated in films, television, and commercials, while tribute acts and stage productions like *We Will Rock You* have kept Queen's music alive for new generations. The success of the 2018 biopic *Bohemian Rhapsody* introduced Queen's story to millions of people worldwide, reigniting interest in the band's music and ensuring that Freddie Mercury's legacy endures.

One of the key reasons for Queen's continued success is the timeless quality of their music. Songs like "Bohemian Rhapsody," "We Will Rock You," and "Don't Stop Me Now" have become cultural anthems, transcending generations and resonating with listeners of all ages. Queen's music has been used in countless films, television shows, and commercials, cementing the band's place in popular culture.

Queen's ability to adapt and evolve over the years, while staying true to the spirit of their music, has been another crucial factor in their longevity. Collaborations with artists like Paul Rodgers and Adam Lambert have allowed the band to reach new audiences, while the re-release of classic albums and the success of *Bohemian Rhapsody* have kept Queen's music at the forefront of popular culture.

THE ENDURING BOND BETWEEN BRIAN MAY AND ROGER TAYLOR

At the heart of Queen's continued success is the enduring friendship and creative partnership between Brian May and Roger Taylor. Throughout the years, the two musicians have remained committed to honoring Freddie's legacy while also continuing to explore new musical possibilities.

Both May and Taylor have pursued solo projects and worked on various collaborations over the years, but their bond as the remaining members of Queen has remained strong. Together, they have navigated the complexities of moving forward without Freddie, while ensuring that Queen's music continues to be celebrated and cherished.

The success of Queen + Adam Lambert has given both May and Taylor a renewed sense of purpose. Performing Queen's iconic songs to sold-out audiences around the world has allowed them to connect with fans who never had the chance to see Queen perform with Freddie, and the experience has been both rewarding and emotional for the band members.

QUEEN'S LEGACY IN THE 21ST CENTURY

As Queen continues to evolve in the 21st century, the band's legacy is more secure than ever. Freddie Mercury's memory remains at the heart of Queen's story, but the band has shown that it can honor the past while also embracing the future. Through collaborations, tribute concerts, and the continued success of their music, Queen's influence is still felt across the world.

Brian May and Roger Taylor have expressed their gratitude for the opportunity to continue sharing Queen's music with new generations of fans, and they remain committed to keeping Queen's legacy alive. For millions of fans around the world, Queen's music continues to inspire, uplift, and unite people, just as it did when Freddie Mercury was leading the band.

Chapter 13:
Collaborations, Tributes, and Films

COLLABORATING WITH OTHER ARTISTS

Even after Freddie Mercury's passing, Queen's influence and reputation in the music industry remained strong. Over the years, Brian May and Roger Taylor collaborated with a variety of contemporary artists across multiple genres, keeping Queen's music alive while introducing it to new audiences.

One of Queen's most notable collaborations in the post-Freddie era was with David Bowie on "Under Pressure" in 1981, but this partnership took on renewed significance after Freddie's death. The track has since become a mainstay in Queen's live performances, both with guest artists like Paul Rodgers and later with Adam Lambert.

In the early 2000s, Queen embarked on a new chapter of collaboration by joining forces with Paul Rodgers. Known for his powerful blues-rock voice, Rodgers was a departure from Freddie Mercury's theatrical and operatic style, but he brought a fresh energy to the band's performances. Together, they toured globally and released an album of original material, *The Cosmos Rocks* (2008), featuring songs that combined Rodgers' bluesy rock influences with Queen's anthemic sound.

However, it was the collaboration with Adam Lambert in 2011 that brought Queen back to center stage in a new and exciting way. Lambert, who gained fame on *American Idol*, had been performing Queen's music for years and seemed a natural fit for the band. His powerful voice, combined with his flamboyant stage presence, drew inevitable comparisons to Freddie Mercury, but Lambert never sought to imitate Freddie. Instead, he brought his own style to the performances, earning praise for his ability to honor Queen's legacy while bringing a modern twist to their iconic songs.

Queen + Adam Lambert embarked on several world tours, performing Queen classics to sold-out arenas and stadiums. Their chemistry, both on stage and off, reinvigorated Queen's music for a new generation of fans. Concerts included powerful renditions of "Bohemian Rhapsody," "Somebody to Love," and "We Will Rock You," with Lambert bringing his own interpretation to Freddie's timeless performances. Critics and audiences alike applauded Lambert's ability to step into such big shoes while maintaining his own identity as a performer.

Beyond live performances, Queen's collaborations with other artists continued to expand through special projects and one-off performances. Brian May and Roger Taylor collaborated with stars like Elton John, Robbie Williams, and Jessie J on various occasions, showing Queen's versatility and enduring appeal across musical genres.

THE WE WILL ROCK YOU MUSICAL

One of the most successful tributes to Queen's music in the 21st century was the *We Will Rock You* musical, which debuted in 2002 at London's Dominion Theatre. Written by Ben Elton and featuring a storyline inspired by Queen's music, the musical was a jukebox-style production that incorporated many of Queen's biggest hits into its narrative.

The plot of *We Will Rock You* was set in a dystopian future where rock music had been outlawed, and a group of rebels, inspired by the spirit of rock, sought to bring music back to the world. While the storyline was secondary to the music, the show became an instant hit, particularly with Queen fans who appreciated the opportunity to hear the band's greatest songs performed live in a theatrical setting.

We Will Rock You ran for an impressive 12 years in London, making it one of the longest-running shows in West End history. It also spawned productions around the world, from Las Vegas to Australia, and the show's success further cemented Queen's place as one of the most beloved bands in rock history.

For Brian May and Roger Taylor, *We Will Rock You* was a new way to keep Queen's music alive in a fresh format. Both members were closely involved in the production, with May occasionally making surprise appearances on stage to perform the guitar solo in "Bohemian Rhapsody." The musical introduced Queen's music to new generations, many of whom may not have been familiar with the band's history, ensuring that Queen's songs would continue to inspire audiences for years to come.

THE BOHEMIAN RHAPSODY FILM (2018)

One of the most significant tributes to Queen and Freddie Mercury came in 2018 with the release of the biographical film *Bohemian Rhapsody*. The film, directed by Bryan Singer and later Dexter Fletcher, chronicled the rise of Queen, focusing on Freddie Mercury's journey from his early days as Farrokh Bulsara to his final years as one of rock's most iconic frontmen.

Rami Malek's portrayal of Freddie Mercury was widely praised, earning him an Academy Award for Best Actor. Malek captured Freddie's charisma, vulnerability, and flamboyance, offering a nuanced and powerful portrayal of a man who defied convention both on and off the stage.

The film took some creative liberties with Queen's history, compressing timelines and embellishing certain aspects of Freddie's life for dramatic effect. For example, the film suggests that Freddie disclosed his HIV diagnosis to the band before their 1985 Live Aid performance, when in reality, he was not diagnosed until later. Despite these liberties, the film resonated deeply with audiences and became a global sensation, grossing over $900 million at the box office.

One of the film's key moments was the recreation of Queen's legendary performance at Live Aid, which served as the climax of the story. The filmmakers meticulously recreated the performance, down to the smallest details, and Rami Malek's portrayal of Freddie during this iconic set captured the essence of what made Queen so electrifying in concert. The film's soundtrack, which featured Queen's greatest hits, once again propelled the band's music to the top of the charts.

For many younger fans, *Bohemian Rhapsody* was their introduction to Queen's music and Freddie Mercury's extraordinary life. The film sparked a renewed interest in Queen's catalog, leading to a surge in streaming and sales of their albums. It also reignited debates about Freddie Mercury's legacy, with fans and critics alike celebrating his courage, talent, and lasting influence on the world of music.

CELEBRATING FREDDIE THROUGH TRIBUTES AND AWARDS

Over the years, Freddie Mercury and Queen have been honored with countless tributes and awards, celebrating their contributions to music and culture. Queen's induction into the Rock and Roll Hall of Fame in 2001 was a significant moment, recognizing their status as one of the most innovative and influential rock bands of all time. During the ceremony, Brian May, Roger Taylor, and John Deacon accepted the award on behalf of the band, with a tribute performance to honor Freddie's memory.

Freddie has also been the subject of numerous tribute concerts, documentaries, and books, each celebrating his immense talent and his impact on both the music industry and LGBTQ+ representation. His flamboyant performances, fearless individuality, and willingness to push boundaries have inspired generations of artists, and his legacy as one of rock's greatest frontmen remains undiminished.

One of the most iconic tributes to Freddie came in 1992 with the Freddie Mercury Tribute Concert for AIDS Awareness, which took place at Wembley Stadium and featured performances from some of the biggest names in music. The concert not only celebrated Freddie's life but also raised millions of pounds for AIDS research, continuing the work that Freddie had quietly supported during his life.

In 1996, a statue of Freddie Mercury was unveiled in Montreux, Switzerland, a place that had become dear to him during the final years of his life. The statue, which overlooks Lake Geneva, has since become a pilgrimage site for Queen fans, who come from all over the world to pay their respects to the man who redefined what it meant to be a rock star.

THE CONTINUING INFLUENCE OF QUEEN'S MUSIC

Queen's music continues to inspire and influence musicians across genres, from rock and pop to classical and electronic music. Their ability to blend different styles—opera, rock, ballads, and even disco—has made Queen one of the most versatile bands in music history. Songs like "Bohemian Rhapsody," "We Will Rock You," and "Don't Stop Me Now" have become cultural anthems, played at sporting events, weddings, parties, and protests alike.

Queen's songs have been covered and reinterpreted by countless artists over the years. From heavy metal bands to pop singers, musicians have been drawn to the complexity, emotion, and sheer energy of Queen's music. Artists like Lady Gaga, Brendon Urie of Panic! At the Disco, and Harry Styles have cited Queen as a major influence on their own music and performances, with many emulating Freddie Mercury's blend of theatricality and raw talent.

The band's continued success in the 21st century, whether through tribute concerts, films, or collaborations with artists like Adam Lambert, is a testament to the timelessness of their music. Even as the music industry changes and evolves, Queen's songs remain as relevant and powerful as ever.

THE ENDURING LEGACY OF BOHEMIAN RHAPSODY

Queen's 1975 hit "Bohemian Rhapsody" remains one of the most iconic songs in music history. The song's unusual structure, blending opera with hard rock, and its mysterious lyrics have fascinated listeners for decades. It became the first song to reach number one on the UK Singles Chart twice (in 1975 and again in 1991, following Freddie's death) and has continued to enjoy success through its appearances in films, commercials, and popular culture.

In 2004, "Bohemian Rhapsody" was inducted into the Grammy Hall of Fame, further cementing its place in music history. The song's impact on the music industry cannot be overstated—it challenged the conventions of radio-friendly rock songs, defied categorization, and became a global phenomenon. The success of the *Bohemian Rhapsody* film in 2018 only reinforced the song's status as a timeless masterpiece.

For Freddie Mercury, "Bohemian Rhapsody" represented his unique vision and willingness to take risks. For Queen, it marked the moment when they fully embraced their individuality and refused to conform to the expectations of the music industry. And for fans, it remains a symbol of Queen's creativity, ambition, and fearless approach to music.

Chapter 14:
The Global Impact of Queen's Music

QUEEN'S POPULARITY IN THE UNITED KINGDOM

From their earliest days, Queen was deeply connected to the British music scene. The band's rise coincided with the emergence of the UK as a global center of rock music, with bands like The Beatles, Led Zeppelin, and The Rolling Stones already shaping the landscape. Queen's ability to blend progressive rock, opera, and theatricality made them stand out, and they quickly became one of the most beloved British rock bands of the 1970s.

Throughout their career, Queen's popularity in the UK never waned. Their first number one single, "Bohemian Rhapsody," spent nine weeks at the top of the UK charts in 1975 and became one of the best-selling singles in British history. Subsequent albums like *A Night at the Opera*, *News of the World*, and *The Game* solidified Queen's place as one of Britain's most successful bands.

The UK also played host to some of Queen's most iconic live performances. Their two shows at Wembley Stadium during the *Magic Tour* in 1986 are often cited as some of the greatest concerts in rock history. These performances, which took place just a year after Queen's legendary Live Aid appearance, drew tens of thousands of fans and further cemented Queen's status as British rock royalty.

Even after Freddie Mercury's passing, Queen's music continued to dominate the British charts. The release of *Bohemian Rhapsody* in 1991 following Freddie's death saw the song return to number one, making Queen the first band to top the UK charts with the same single in different decades. The band's enduring popularity in the UK is reflected in the continued success of their albums, compilations, and reissues, as well as the widespread love for the *We Will Rock You* musical.

QUEEN'S IMPACT IN THE UNITED STATES

Queen's journey in the United States was initially slower compared to their explosive success in the UK. While their earlier albums performed well in the US, it wasn't until the release of *News of the World* in 1977 that Queen achieved widespread success across the Atlantic. The anthems "We Will Rock You" and "We Are the Champions" became staples of American sports arenas, and their unique sound resonated with a wide range of listeners.

By the late 1970s, Queen was headlining massive arenas in the US, and their album *The Game* (1980) solidified their popularity with hits like "Another One Bites the Dust" and "Crazy Little Thing Called Love." "Another One Bites the Dust," in particular, became Queen's biggest hit in the US, topping the Billboard Hot 100 chart and making Queen a household name.

However, the band's popularity in the US faced challenges in the early 1980s, particularly after the release of *Hot Space* (1982), which incorporated disco and funk elements that didn't resonate as strongly with American rock fans. Nevertheless, Queen's fan base remained loyal, and their legendary performance at Live Aid in 1985 helped reignite their popularity in the US.

After Freddie Mercury's death, Queen's influence in the United States only grew. The release of the *Bohemian Rhapsody* film in 2018 reintroduced Queen to a new generation of American fans, and their collaboration with Adam Lambert has allowed the band to tour extensively across North America, performing to sold-out arenas and festivals.

QUEEN'S CULTURAL IMPACT IN JAPAN

Japan has long been one of Queen's most devoted markets. The band first toured Japan in 1975 after the release of *Sheer Heart Attack*, and they were met with an overwhelming reception. Japanese fans were captivated by Queen's theatrical performances and their eclectic blend of musical styles. Freddie Mercury's flamboyant stage presence, in particular, resonated with Japanese audiences, who embraced his larger-than-life persona.

Japan quickly became one of Queen's most important international markets, and the band enjoyed a level of adulation in the country that rivaled their fame in the UK. Queen's albums consistently performed well on Japanese charts, and their tours in the country were sell-outs, with fans greeting them like superstars.

Freddie Mercury's love for Japan was well-known, and he often spoke of his deep connection to Japanese culture. He was a collector of Japanese art and antiques, and the influence of Japan can be seen in some of Queen's music and visual aesthetic. The song "Teo Torriatte (Let Us Cling Together)" from *A Day at the Races* is a tribute to the band's Japanese fans, with parts of the song sung in Japanese.

Even after Freddie's death, Queen's popularity in Japan remained strong. The band's albums and compilations have continued to perform well in the country, and Queen + Adam Lambert's tours have been met with enthusiastic responses from Japanese audiences. Queen's influence on Japanese rock and pop music is significant, with many Japanese artists citing Queen as a major influence on their sound and performance style.

QUEEN'S INFLUENCE IN LATIN AMERICA

Queen's global reach extended to Latin America in the early 1980s, when they became one of the first major rock bands to tour the region. Their 1981 tour of Argentina, Brazil, and Mexico was a groundbreaking moment for rock music in Latin America, where few Western bands had ventured before. The tour was a massive success, with Queen playing to record-breaking crowds, including an audience of over 300,000 in São Paulo, Brazil, one of the largest rock concerts in history.

Queen's music resonated deeply with Latin American audiences, who were drawn to the band's blend of rock, opera, and dramatic flair. Songs like "Love of My Life" became particularly beloved in the region, with fans often singing along to every word during Queen's live performances. Freddie Mercury's ability to connect with audiences, even those who didn't speak English, made Queen's concerts in Latin America some of the most memorable of their career.

Queen's influence in Latin America has remained strong in the decades since their 1981 tour. The band's music continues to be popular across the region, and Queen + Adam Lambert have performed to enthusiastic crowds in cities like Buenos Aires, Rio de Janeiro, and São Paulo. The success of the *Bohemian Rhapsody* film also reintroduced Queen's music to a new generation of Latin American fans, ensuring that the band's legacy continues to thrive in the region.

QUEEN'S REACH ACROSS EUROPE

In Europe, Queen has long been one of the most popular and influential bands in rock history. From the early days of their career, Queen's music resonated with European audiences, and their tours across the continent helped cement their status as one of the world's greatest live acts.

In countries like Germany, the Netherlands, France, and Italy, Queen's music became deeply ingrained in popular culture. Their albums consistently topped European charts, and their live performances drew massive crowds. Queen's unique ability to blend rock with elements of classical music, opera, and pop gave them broad appeal across Europe, where audiences were more open to experimental and genre-bending sounds.

Queen's popularity in Eastern Europe was also significant, particularly during the 1980s when they became one of the few Western rock bands to perform in countries behind the Iron Curtain. Their 1986 concert in Budapest, Hungary, was a landmark event, as it marked the first time a major rock band from the West had performed in the Eastern Bloc. The concert, which was filmed and later released as *Queen: Live in Budapest*, was attended by over 80,000 fans and became a symbol of the growing cultural exchanges between East and West during the final years of the Cold War.

Even after Freddie's death, Queen's music has remained a cultural touchstone across Europe. The band's albums continue to be best-sellers, and their music is often featured in films, commercials, and sporting events. The continued success of Queen + Adam Lambert has allowed European audiences to experience Queen's music live once again, with tours regularly selling out arenas and stadiums across the continent.

THE UNIVERSAL APPEAL OF QUEEN'S MUSIC

Queen's ability to transcend borders, languages, and cultures is one of the defining aspects of their legacy. While their music is deeply rooted in British rock, Queen's eclectic blend of genres—from classical and opera to rock, pop, and funk—has given them a universal appeal that resonates with audiences around the world.

Freddie Mercury's theatricality, powerful voice, and stage presence made Queen's live performances unforgettable, and his ability to connect with audiences of all backgrounds helped the band achieve global success. Songs like "We Are the Champions," "Bohemian Rhapsody," and "Radio Ga Ga" have become anthems not just for rock fans, but for people from all walks of life.

Queen's music continues to be a unifying force, bringing people together through its timeless appeal and emotional power. Whether performed in a sold-out stadium, heard in a film or commercial, or sung by fans at a sporting event, Queen's songs have the ability to inspire, uplift, and entertain like few other bands in history.

QUEEN'S ENDURING GLOBAL LEGACY

As Queen enters its fifth decade of global influence, the band's legacy shows no signs of fading. Their music has touched millions of lives, spanning generations, and continues to inspire musicians, performers, and fans around the world. From their early days in London to their sold-out tours with Adam Lambert, Queen's impact on the world of music remains unparalleled.

Queen's global legacy is not only defined by their music but also by their message of individuality, creativity, and defiance of convention. Freddie Mercury, in particular, became a symbol of self-expression and authenticity, inspiring people to embrace who they are, regardless of societal expectations. His fearlessness in the face of personal and professional challenges remains an inspiration to countless fans around the world.

As Queen's music continues to be celebrated in films, concerts, and tribute performances, their influence will undoubtedly endure for many years to come. The global impact of Queen's music, combined with their boundary-pushing creativity and ability to connect with audiences, ensures that Queen will remain one of the most iconic and beloved bands in rock history.

Chapter 15:
Queen's Lasting Influence On Music And Popular Culture

QUEEN'S IMPACT ON FUTURE ARTISTS

Queen's influence on the music industry has been profound, inspiring countless artists across a wide array of genres. Freddie Mercury's powerful voice, stage presence, and ability to blend different styles of music were groundbreaking, and many artists have drawn inspiration from his unique approach to performance and songwriting.

One of the most notable aspects of Queen's influence is their genre-defying approach to music. Queen seamlessly blended rock with opera, classical music, disco, and pop, creating a distinctive sound that broke away from the conventions of typical rock bands. This willingness to experiment with different genres influenced future musicians who sought to push boundaries and explore new artistic directions.

Artists like Lady Gaga, who took her stage name from Queen's hit "Radio Ga Ga," have credited Queen as a major influence on their careers. Lady Gaga's theatrical performances, larger-than-life persona, and blending of pop with other genres have drawn frequent comparisons to Freddie Mercury's flamboyance and versatility. She has often spoken about how Queen's music empowered her to embrace her individuality and take risks in her own career.

Similarly, pop-rock artists like Brendon Urie of Panic! At the Disco have cited Queen as a key influence on their sound and stage presence. Urie, known for his powerful vocal range and theatrical performances, often incorporates elements of Queen's grandeur into his own music. His performance style and showmanship draw clear parallels to the over-the-top performances that Queen popularized during the 1970s and 1980s.

Rock bands such as Muse and The Killers have also been heavily influenced by Queen's expansive soundscapes and theatrical elements. Muse, in particular, has often been compared to Queen for their grandiose live performances, multi-layered harmonies, and complex musical arrangements. Their ability to blend progressive rock with symphonic elements has earned them a reputation as one of the most Queen-inspired bands of the 21st century.

In addition to rock and pop artists, Queen's influence can be felt in hip-hop and electronic music. Songs like "Another One Bites the Dust" and "Under Pressure" have been widely sampled by hip-hop artists, highlighting Queen's broad appeal beyond rock. The iconic bassline of "Another One Bites the Dust" became a blueprint for many hip-hop tracks in the 1980s and 1990s, showcasing how Queen's music transcended genre boundaries and influenced a wide range of musical styles.

QUEEN'S ENDURING LEGACY IN FILM, TELEVISION, AND ADVERTISING

Queen's music has also become a fixture in films, television, and advertising, further embedding their songs into popular culture. From *Wayne's World* to *Bohemian Rhapsody*, Queen's music has been featured in countless iconic moments on screen, ensuring that their songs remain relevant to audiences of all generations.

One of the most famous examples of Queen's music in film is the unforgettable scene in *Wayne's World* (1992) where the characters, played by Mike Myers and Dana Carvey, perform an air-guitar singalong to "Bohemian

Rhapsody" in a car. The scene became a cultural phenomenon and introduced the song to a new generation of fans. After the film's release, "Bohemian Rhapsody" returned to the charts, and Queen's music enjoyed a resurgence in popularity in the early 1990s.

Queen's anthems are frequently used in sports arenas, commercials, and television shows, making them a ubiquitous part of popular culture. Songs like "We Will Rock You" and "We Are the Champions" have become synonymous with victory, triumph, and celebration. They are often played at major sporting events, including the Olympics and the World Cup, cementing their place as universal rallying cries.

Television talent shows such as *The X Factor* and *American Idol* have regularly featured Queen's music, with contestants often choosing Queen songs to showcase their vocal abilities. These performances have introduced Queen's music to younger audiences, keeping their legacy alive in the digital age. Queen's songs, with their challenging vocal ranges and dynamic energy, have become go-to choices for contestants looking to make a memorable impression.

In advertising, Queen's music has been used to sell everything from cars to smartphones. Their powerful anthems and universally appealing lyrics have made them a favorite choice for brands looking to convey messages of confidence, innovation, and success. Whether through a sports ad featuring "We Will Rock You" or a nostalgic commercial set to "Don't Stop Me Now," Queen's music has remained a timeless soundtrack for countless marketing campaigns.

THE INFLUENCE OF FREDDIE MERCURY AS A CULTURAL ICON

Beyond Queen's music, Freddie Mercury himself has become a cultural icon whose influence extends far beyond the world of rock. His flamboyant stage presence, unapologetic individuality, and fearless approach to life have made him a symbol of freedom, creativity, and authenticity.

Freddie Mercury's impact on LGBTQ+ representation in music cannot be overstated. Although Freddie never officially came out as gay or bisexual during his lifetime, his visibility as an LGBTQ+ figure helped pave the way for future artists to express their identities openly. Freddie's flamboyant persona, gender-fluid fashion, and celebration of self-expression made him a trailblazer for the LGBTQ+ community, inspiring generations of artists and fans to embrace their true selves.

Freddie's bold fashion choices, from his glamorous outfits in the 1970s to his iconic leather looks in the 1980s, left a lasting impact on the world of fashion. His daring style, which often blurred the lines between masculinity and femininity, challenged societal norms and continues to influence designers and musicians alike. Freddie's signature look—a white tank top, mustache, and armband—has become iconic, symbolizing both his stage presence and his place as a cultural icon.

Freddie's influence also extends to the way he approached his illness in the final years of his life. His decision to keep his HIV/AIDS diagnosis private, while controversial to some, allowed him to continue focusing on his music and his passion for life without being defined by his illness. Freddie's eventual public acknowledgment of his illness, just days before his death, helped raise awareness about AIDS and contributed to destigmatizing the disease at a time when it was still misunderstood.

For many, Freddie Mercury represents the ultimate rock star—a performer who embraced risk, broke boundaries, and lived life to the fullest. His legacy as one of the greatest vocalists and performers in rock history is undisputed, and his influence on music, culture, and LGBTQ+ representation continues to grow.

THE LEGACY OF QUEEN'S LIVE PERFORMANCES

One of the hallmarks of Queen's career has always been their live performances. From their early days performing in small clubs to headlining stadiums around the world, Queen earned a reputation as one of the greatest live bands of all time. Freddie Mercury's magnetic stage presence, combined with Brian May's virtuosic guitar playing and Roger Taylor's powerful drumming, made Queen's concerts unforgettable experiences for their audiences.

The 1985 Live Aid performance at Wembley Stadium is often hailed as Queen's greatest live moment and is regarded by many as one of the greatest live performances in rock history. In just 20 minutes, Queen captivated a global audience of millions with a setlist that included "Bohemian Rhapsody," "Radio Ga Ga," and "We Will Rock You." Freddie's interaction with the crowd, particularly during the call-and-response "Ay-oh!" segment, demonstrated his unparalleled ability to engage an audience.

Even after Freddie's death, Queen's live legacy has continued. Collaborations with Paul Rodgers and Adam Lambert have allowed Brian May and Roger Taylor to keep performing Queen's music live for new generations of fans. Lambert's voice and stage presence, in particular, have been praised for capturing the spirit of Queen's music, while bringing a fresh interpretation to their classic songs.

Queen's live performances, whether with Freddie or their later collaborations, have set a benchmark for other bands to aspire to. Their ability to connect with audiences, deliver powerful musical moments, and create unforgettable spectacles has made Queen's live shows legendary.

QUEEN'S INFLUENCE ON THE MUSIC INDUSTRY

Queen's innovation in music production, stagecraft, and music videos has left a lasting impact on the music industry. Their use of multi-tracked vocals, layered guitar effects, and elaborate studio techniques set new standards for recording technology in rock music. Brian May's development of his own guitar sound using homemade equipment, combined with Freddie's insistence on pushing the boundaries of what was possible in the studio, influenced future generations of producers and musicians.

The groundbreaking music video for "Bohemian Rhapsody," released in 1975, is often credited with ushering in the modern era of music videos. The video's striking imagery, including the iconic shot of the band members in silhouette, helped establish the visual language of rock videos and paved the way for the music video boom of the 1980s, when MTV became a dominant force in popular culture. Queen's ability to use visuals to enhance their music set a precedent for future artists to follow.

Queen's approach to songwriting also influenced how bands thought about structure, form, and experimentation. The success of songs like "Bohemian Rhapsody," which defied conventional song structure, encouraged other artists to take risks in their songwriting and to challenge industry expectations about what makes a hit song.

Queen's willingness to embrace different genres, from opera and classical to disco and funk, opened the door for other artists to experiment and expand the boundaries of rock music. Their fearlessness in blending styles has become a blueprint for many artists who refuse to be confined by genre labels.

QUEEN'S TIMELESS APPEAL

As Queen's music continues to inspire new generations of fans, it's clear that their legacy will endure for many years to come. Their songs, performances, and cultural influence have transcended time and continue to resonate with audiences of all ages. Queen's music is timeless, offering something for everyone—whether it's the operatic grandeur of "Bohemian Rhapsody," the defiant anthem of "We Will Rock You," or the joyous celebration of life in "Don't Stop Me Now."

For millions of people around the world, Queen's music represents the power of creativity, individuality, and the belief that music can bring people together. Freddie Mercury's legacy as a cultural icon, combined with the band's musical innovations and electrifying performances, has ensured that Queen's place in the pantheon of rock's greatest bands is secure.

As the curtain closes on Queen's remarkable journey, one thing remains certain: Queen's influence on music, culture, and the world at large will continue to grow, inspiring future generations to embrace their creativity, challenge the status quo, and live life with the same fearlessness that defined Freddie Mercury and Queen.

Here is a comprehensive list of all the singles and albums by both Queen and Freddie Mercury.

Queen: Studio Albums
1. Queen (1973)
2. Queen II (1974)
3. Sheer Heart Attack (1974)
4. A Night at the Opera (1975)
5. A Day at the Races (1976)
6. News of the World (1977)
7. Jazz (1978)
8. The Game (1980)
9. Flash Gordon (Soundtrack) (1980)
10. Hot Space (1982)
11. The Works (1984)
12. A Kind of Magic (1986)
13. The Miracle (1989)
14. Innuendo (1991)
15. Made in Heaven (1995)

Queen: Live Albums
1. Live Killers (1979)
2. Live Magic (1986)
3. Live at Wembley '86 (1992)
4. Queen on Fire – Live at the Bowl (2004)
5. Queen Rock Montreal (2007)
6. Hungarian Rhapsody: Queen Live in Budapest (2012)
7. A Night at the Odeon (2015)

Queen: Compilation Albums
1. Greatest Hits (1981)
2. Greatest Hits II (1991)
3. Greatest Hits III (1999)
4. Queen Forever (2014)

Freddie Mercury: Studio Albums (Solo)

1. Mr. Bad Guy (1985)
2. Barcelona (with Montserrat Caballé) (1988)

Freddie Mercury: Compilation Albums (Solo)

1. The Freddie Mercury Album (1992)
2. The Solo Collection (2000)
3. Lover of Life, Singer of Songs (2006)
4. Messenger of the Gods: The Singles (2016)

Queen: Notable Singles

1. Keep Yourself Alive (1973)
2. Seven Seas of Rhye (1974)
3. Killer Queen (1974)
4. Now I'm Here (1974)
5. Bohemian Rhapsody (1975)
6. You're My Best Friend (1976)
7. Somebody to Love (1976)
8. Tie Your Mother Down (1977)
9. We Are the Champions/We Will Rock You (1977)
10. Fat Bottomed Girls/Bicycle Race (1978)
11. Don't Stop Me Now (1979)
12. Crazy Little Thing Called Love (1979)
13. Another One Bites the Dust (1980)
14. Flash (1980)
15. Under Pressure (with David Bowie) (1981)
16. Radio Ga Ga (1984)
17. I Want to Break Free (1984)
18. Hammer to Fall (1984)
19. A Kind of Magic (1986)
20. Who Wants to Live Forever (1986)
21. I Want It All (1989)
22. Breakthru (1989)
23. The Miracle (1989)
24. Innuendo (1991)

25. The Show Must Go On (1991)

26. These Are the Days of Our Lives (1991)

Freddie Mercury: Notable Singles (Solo)

1. Love Kills (1984)
2. I Was Born to Love You (1985)
3. Living on My Own (1985)
4. Made in Heaven (1985)
5. Barcelona (with Montserrat Caballé) (1987)
6. The Great Pretender (1987)
7. How Can I Go On (with Montserrat Caballé) (1988)
8. In My Defence (1992)
9. Living on My Own (No More Brothers Mix) (1993)
10. Love Me Like There's No Tomorrow (1985)

Queen: Notable Posthumous Singles

1. Too Much Love Will Kill You (1995)
2. Let Me Live (1996)
3. Heaven for Everyone (1995)
4. A Winter's Tale (1995)

Notable Concerts by Queen

1. Live Aid (Wembley Stadium, London) – July 13, 1985
2. Rock in Rio Festival (Rio de Janeiro, Brazil) – January 1985
3. Wembley Stadium (Magic Tour, London) – July 11 & 12, 1986
4. Live in Budapest – July 27, 1986
5. Queen's 1981 South American Tour (Argentina, Brazil)
6. Montreal Forum (1981, filmed as *Queen Rock Montreal*)
7. Queen at Hyde Park – September 18, 1976
8. Queen at Hammersmith Odeon – December 24, 1975

This comprehensive list covers Queen and Freddie Mercury's major albums, singles, and notable concerts. It showcases Queen's phenomenal journey from their early albums to Freddie's final work, as well as his solo ventures.

Printed in Great Britain
by Amazon

61355591R00050